PRAISE FOR
COUNTRY BOY, CITY BOY

"James Cooley has shared his story of struggle and success in America as both a cautionary tale and a roadmap to achieving the 'American Dream.' As an African-American, his autobiography is firmly in the tradition of Richard Wright, James Baldwin, and Ralph Ellison, portraying the dire disadvantages faced by those growing up poor and black in America. But don't expect to find bitter invective about systemic 'White Oppression.' As a retired high school English teacher, I believe that his first-hand account of the spiritual and intellectual maturation that fueled his escape from cyclical poverty should be required reading in America's secondary schools."

—Derry R. Van Nortwick, M.A.

"There's much truth in 'a journey that ain't over yet,' as all of us journey through life's precious gift of time, and James Cooley did so with the love and guidance he received from his beloved mother and grandmother that made this journey successful. Traversing from the country life to city life and from the outhouse to the White House... [this] book clearly demonstrated James Cooley's preparedness to tackle opportunities presented to him."

—Knot Souimaniphanh, Colonel, United States Army

"It is an inspiration to follow his life from living in the poor city life of Chattanooga, Tennessee, and the poor country life of Graham, Alabama, to becoming a successful Navy career as an officer, working as a design engineer at the Pentagon, and eventually establishing his own foundation for inspiring youths and young adults to see another path. James not only gives us insight to what led himself to the great place he's arrived at but reminds us that he's not finished with his work and he still has much more to accomplish. He wants us to think big, just as he has done throughout his whole life, leading as an example, and never giving up, as could have easily happened anywhere along his own life's path."

—Max Cantu, retired high school teacher
and administrator

"Whether as a career Naval officer serving our nation, a business leader, or the CEO of his nonprofit, JC has been a beaming light of hope and encouragement. In *Country Boy, City Boy: A Journey That Ain't Over Yet*, he shares his unfiltered truth to provide hope for the future by challenging readers to refuse to become victims of life's circumstance and encouraging them to dare to be overcomers because a bigger, better and more impactful life awaits them."

—Herman L. Archibald, Captain (retired),
United States Navy

"This book has a majestic ability to trigger nostalgic childhood memories, learning the meaning of hard work and sacrifice and the importance of earning a good education. *Country Boy, City Boy: A Journey That Ain't Over Yet* encapsulates life's prerequisites towards pursuing the 'American Dream.'"

—Shon Moore, Colonel, United States Army

"James Cooley's personal and poignant family stories will inspire and make you laugh. A Navy career that stresses the importance of education, training and mentorship. A life experience full of philosophies and achievements uniquely focused now on teaching leadership skills to teenagers."

—M. Hayden, Marketing and Sales Executive (retired)

"From his frank introduction to his very colorful descriptions of his early life on the farm, Mr. Cooley draws you into his world, which is both poignant and fascinating simultaneously."

—Dr. Lester A. Freeman, Pediatrician

"The story James Cooley tells is one of triumph and profound achievement in the midst of childhood adversity and community dysfunction. It is a personal revelation that is inspiring and uplifting. A must read."

—Gwen Wright, National Playwright and Author

"James Cooley offers a compelling story of success. It would have been easy for him to fall into the pattern of most of those around and perpetuate the lifestyle. Led by his intelligence and his faith he chose a different path."

—Sandy Dodson, retired business owner

"An enjoyable insight into one man's life journey, sprinkled with humor and humble storytelling, make this a wonderful read. A moving reminder that through life's twists, trials, and triumphs we find inspiration that leads to our destiny and God's plan."

—V. Parker, Senior HR Business Partner

Country Boy, City Boy:
A Journey That Ain't Over Yet

by James Cooley

© Copyright 2019 James Cooley

ISBN 978-1-63393-907-3

All rights reserved. No part of this publication may be reproduced, stored in a retrieval system, or transmitted in any form or by any means—electronic, mechanical, photocopy, recording, or any other—except for brief quotations in printed reviews, without the prior written permission of the author.

Published by

CooleyBooks
Email address: jamescooley145@gmail.com
Phone number: 817-729-6272

This book is dedicated to the women who had the most influence in my upbringing and in shaping the person I am today. Grandma (Mattie Blake Stephens), you guided me through the earliest years of my life. I will always remember the love, attention and, most importantly, the many words of wisdom that you instilled in my heart and mind that all people are good people until they show you otherwise Grandma, I miss you so much. You are my inspiration for everything that I do on this Earth.

Mama (Gladys Stephens), I always think about you and all of the love you gave to me when I felt like I was out of place in life. Mama, thanks for having the faith and confidence to choose me and Jerry to live in Alabama with Uncle Robert and Aunt Geneva. They instilled in me values, confidence and a solid work ethic. I miss you Mama. You will always be there, with every thought and every second that I have left on this Earth. I love you Mama.

COUNTRY BOY, CITY BOY

A Journey that Ain't Over Yet

JAMES COOLEY

TABLE OF CONTENTS

Introduction 1

Part I: The Country................................. 5
    Lucky No. 7
    Survival 11
    Never Know What You Will Pull Out of a Well ... 15
    There Can Only Be One Rooster................ 18
    The Schoolhouse and Stephens 21
    Family Tree 26

Part II: The City................................... 29
    Country Boy, City Boy 31
    That White Woman Done Lost Her Mind 35
    Nobody's Baby Daddy 41
    A Steak Cut Right Down the Middle 44

Part III: The Navy 49
    Welcome to the Navy 51
    Points of Light 57
    Leading by Example........................... 62
    Commander, You're on the Fat Boy Program ... 66
    From the Outhouse to the White House 71
    Timeline of My Navy Career................... 77

Part IV: A New Path 81
    Soaring to New Heights....................... 83
    Repairing Old Wounds 86
    Daring to Dream Big, Think Big, and Be Big 95

Part V: My Philosophies 103
    Introduction to My Philosophies: The 6 T's. . . . 105
    Focus Is Key. 109
    Our Birthrights 111
    The 4 C's 113
    ACE 115
    LIFE. 117
    87/10/3 119
    A Strong Foundation 122
    A Start and a Finish Date 124
    The Choice 127
    Pssssst . . . You Are a Masterpiece 128

Part VI: Reflections: Yesterday, Today,
        and Tomorrow 131

Acknowledgments. 136

INTRODUCTION

When I was thirty, I told myself I was going to write a book. That was when I started to see, with eyes more open with some distance and age, the dynamics of my life in both the rural Deep South and in a poor, urban neighborhood 150 miles north.

These dynamics looked like this: My mother, who never married, had ten children by six different fathers. At one point, my mother, my father's wife, and my oldest sister were all expecting babies at the same time. Twice, my mother and my two older sisters were pregnant at the same time. And within my larger family circle, circumstances also led to first cousins who were half-sisters. I'm still trying to figure out what to call that, besides saying we had family members who were multiple kin.

This is what poverty, lack of education, and helplessness looks like—the feeling of being destined to repeat the same pattern of our mammas or daddies, if we were lucky enough to have one around, our brothers or sisters, our aunts or uncles. It was the same story, over and over, just as we would rise before dawn every day on our Alabama farm and begin chopping wood and feeding the animals. The sun would set on us doing the same thing.

Every sunrise. Every sunset. Because that's how we survived. Same old thing, each day, which led to many of us dropping out of school.

The projects where my mother and siblings lived in the city, we also had a predetermined life—girls were lucky to turn sixteen and not be pregnant; the boys were lucky to call themselves high school graduates.

Generation after generation, that happened because it was the only way we knew.

I felt a need to write this reality down, to explore why this happened and not have any lessons or meaning I could take from it fade over time. I realized time may have moved on elsewhere, but in these Southern areas it is still very much stuck in the past.

In my forties, I thought again about writing a book as I was leaving a twenty-three-year career in the United States military that took me around the world and to the highest levels of service.

As my experiences varied and deepened, the thought was like a reoccurring drumbeat. As I write this now with nearly sixty years under my belt, I feel I might have had eight or nine lives.

In my youth, I was a country boy and a city boy, experiencing two worlds in the South.

To escape the pull of poverty that gripped us so tight we couldn't see beyond it, I joined the US Navy, rising to become a commissioned officer and serving in the Pentagon.

I also dabbled in acting and comedy, exploring a side to me that loved talking, cracking jokes, and making the other team laugh (I guess I was voted "Class Clown" in high school for a reason), though I quickly found that lifestyle wasn't for me.

I have been an aerospace engineer for the government and one of the top-ranking African-American aerospace engineers at Lockheed Martin.

Along the way, I came to realize how important education is. To this day, the idea of learning and growing forms the foundation of my beliefs about how to achieve success. I hold a total of twelve degrees and master's level certificates; always a student, I'm currently working on my doctorate in education in organizational leadership. When I look at where I came from, it was a tremendous feat for me to even envision earning these degrees and academic achievements.

I was compelled to share my story and some of the wisdom I've been able to gain on this path. I became a motivational speaker and founded a nonprofit organization, The JC Cooley Foundation–Options & Opportunities: The Choice Program, to inspire youths and teens and to help them become future leaders, however that looks for them.

I hope my experiences will help you envision what's possible and realize what you can achieve. I hope this book will be a companion for you on your journey.

As for me, if I've learned anything in the almost six decades of life God has blessed me with, it's this: My journey ain't over yet.

A final thought: The following pages capture my recollections, with the great help of family members and friends who have lent their time and memories. I have sought to accurately portray the details this book contains to the best of my ability and to capture the reality of these experiences and my upbringing as it looked to me.

JAMES COOLEY
Temecula, California

PART I:
THE COUNTRY

When the rooster crowed, we knew it was time to start gathering the eggs from the chicken house and get the water from the well. Time to make sure the hogs had some slop, the chickens had feed, and our mule, Big Red, had his hay and some water.

—my morning chores on our farm in Graham, Alabama

LUCKY NO. 7

The 1959 Chevy Bel Air carrying me from the city of Chattanooga bounced slowly down the long dirt road as we got closer to my new home deep in the woods of Alabama. We passed towering oak trees and elms that covered the sky above us with thick green canopies.

The trees above the road that led me to a new home in Graham, Alabama and a new path in life.

Er continued through the quietness of the sixty-six acres of farm and pasture, quiet except for the peck, peck, peck of the chickens and the low grunts of the hogs and the gentle gurgle of the creek where I would wade and catch frogs and scurry from the black racer snakes.

In the projects where I lived before with my mama and my nine siblings, we'd hear babies crying, adults arguing, and shouting that grew into stabbings or worse—day after day it seemed. The Chevy was carrying me away from that to new sounds and to my brother Jerry, who was older by fifteen months and had been sent to live with Aunt Geneva and Uncle Robert on the family farm months earlier.

My journey had started with a visit from my mama's oldest sister, Aunt Bert, and my cousin Minnie and her four pretty teenage daughters, who looked just like The Supremes.

"Oh, Junior, you're so cuuute!" my cousins had cooed while pinching and kissing my chubby six-year-old cheeks. I had looked up at them with coy eyes and a little smile, and they kept pinching and praising. I think I would have gone anywhere just to keep that comin'.

Meanwhile, Mama and Aunt Bert had been deep in conversation, eventually breaking away to ask me a question that would send me two hours south and in a different direction for the rest of my life.

"Junior," Aunt Bert said in a Southern drawl that comes from deep country living, "why dontcha come back with me?"

Even at that young age, I knew how dangerous our neighborhood was. I swear, God's honest truth, I'd seen one of my mother's boyfriends twice shoot a man in the middle of the street. What happened afterwards I don't recall, though the police rarely came out if they were even called at all.

I also knew that my mother knew she could no longer take care of all ten of us.

My first picture in Graham, Alabama when I was six years old (1965)

So when they asked me that question—a huge one for a child of any age much less six years old—I didn't think much of it. I was an outgoing and curious kid, and it sounded like a hell of an adventure. Plus, my pretty cousins were lovin' on me, as they would do on the entire ride down. As we made our way to Alabama, I didn't really notice much else until we got to those tall trees that led us down the path to the weathered clapboard cottage where I'd live with Aunt Gen, Uncle Robert, Grandma Mattie, and Jerry.

The five of us would share this two-bedroom home surrounded by tall grass and thick vines where we had water hand-drawn from our well and heated by a wood-burning stove, an outhouse for a bathroom, and a candle and kerosene for light.

My Alabama family welcomed me and called me Junior after my father or June Bug because I liked to catch those big beetles and put them in jelly jars. I had my cousins and attention and room to roam and explore. Additionally, the brotherly bond is strong. Jerry and I giggled like little girls when we were reunited, just as we did later when we sent a roll of Charmin toilet paper streaming down the long pasture leading to our outhouse to figure out how many sheets it had. (We got it about halfway unrolled before Uncle Robert saw us and quickly whipped our butts.)

The house where I grew up in Graham, Alabama

On December 1, 1965, I became a member of this town of Graham, Alabama, along the Georgia-Alabama state line, where maybe 200 souls call home today.

Here, we'd make our *own* heat. We had our *own* land and woods and pasture to explore. We had our *own* food from our trees of peaches, walnuts, and pecans or from our fields of peanuts, potatoes, and tomatoes.

Here, there were no more gunshots. There was no more sharing a room with four of my brothers. No more rushing home at night to get something to eat before it was all gone.

After five or six days in my new home, I felt rich.

Originally, Gladys Stephens left Graham, Alabama, with three children in tow and another on the way to follow a boyfriend who had a job in Chattanooga. There she met my father and eventually found another boyfriend who would become the father of her last three children.

Because my mother had three kids by her boyfriend before me, and three kids by her boyfriend after me, I felt like the black since my father never came around. My father, a preacher man named James Bradford who was widely known in our Tennessee community for his charisma and having the light of the Lord in his eyes. I believe she loved him deeply and me too; in some ways I was a mama's boy. But my brothers and sisters saw me as different.

With no education or money and many mouths to feed, my mother had ended up in a public housing project, the Spencer J. McCallie Homes, where more than 600 families and roaches and rats all lived together.

Gladys was a hardworking woman with soft doe eyes who had two, sometimes three jobs. Working as a maid at a hotel, for a doctor in his home, or as a cook in a restaurant, she did whatever she had to, good, bad, or indifferent, to get by and take care of her children. We lived in a four-bedroom unit where she always had a male visitor or boyfriend and always, always had a cigarette lit.

My youngest sister, Gail, recalls she also had an open heart and home. Friends, acquaintances, or anyone in need in the neighborhood could come stay in our little place that was already busting at the seams.

We ate with the help of food stamps and had running water and electricity given to us by the city.

While my father and his family of four children would occupy a part of my life, at times a small one, at other times a bigger part, he has always remained somewhat of a mystery to me.

I'm not sure when Gladys Stephens decided it was all too much for her or how she went down the list of her children to decide who to send to her sisters, though I've often wondered. I just know I ended up being lucky number seven.

SURVIVAL

When I called Graham, Alabama, home, it had an old cotton gin, Butler's Mill, that'd been built in 1912, and a couple of little stores that still remain, and a one-room schoolhouse, and a Methodist church, and not much else. It wasn't until recently that it was even on a map.

This little outpost also had a lot of descendants of the Stephens family. At least 75 percent were my kin, I believe. We're pretty sure that my grandfather Robert Stephens got the farm under the forty acres and a mule promise, which gave black folks some land and a mule to make up for slavery in some small part. He got the last name Stephens, we're pretty sure, because his former owners were called Stephens and it was a common practice to name slaves after their owners. Pretty much everyone in this tiny town had been owned by the Stephenses or were a Stephens. When Robert Stephens married

My grandparents Robert Stephens and Mattie Blake Stephens in the early 1930's

my grandmother, Mattie Blake, he already had seventeen children, a number that would grow to twenty-one with her.

It might have been 1965, but I remember life there was just like that TV show *Little House on the Prairie* about a pioneer family on a Minnesota farm almost 100 years earlier.

Our entire day was structured around our survival. It was also that way in the projects—we just went about it differently.

Food was the first priority. At four a.m., Uncle Robert or Aunt Gen would get me and Jerry up from the room we shared with them so we could get in a couple hours of work before the bus picked us up for school.

When the rooster crowed, we knew it was time to start gathering the eggs from the chicken house and get the water from the well. Time to make sure the hogs had some slop, the chickens had feed, and our mule, Big Red, had his hay and some water.

We'd go out and nab a rabbit, or possum, or squirrel. They had no chance against us, two young, hungry, and crafty boys. We'd catch bullfrogs from the springs that ran along the farm and cut off their legs or grab a gigantic turtle, cracking its shell open with a hammer to make the most delicious soup you'd ever have.

We'd walk into the pasture and crawl up an apple or apricot tree and grab a piece of the sweetest fruit you'd ever taste or a handful of pecans or walnuts. We'd pick corn, peanuts, cabbage, and "ice" potatoes, what we in the South call those white Idaho potatoes, from our fields.

In Tennessee back in the projects, nothing was expected of us. But here we knew as loud and as clear as that rooster's morning wake-up call what we had to do.

We'd return from school by four p.m. and get to work all over again until we got what we needed in order to get by through the night and the next morning.

It didn't stop, because that's what we had to do in order to survive.

We learned to tolerate the bug bites and other small hazards of country life with a remedy Southerners swore by: snuff. Everyone rolled cigarettes with it or dipped it, or both. Uncle Robert, Aunt Gen, Grandma Mattie—they'd all put a pinch of the loose tobacco in between their lip and cheek, spitting the juice with precision as they worked in the field or sat on the front porch.

They'd also rub it on almost anything that pained you.

Got a bee sting? They'd pull you over, take a bit from their mouth, and thirty to forty minutes later, the pain was gone.

Arthritis? A sore knee? Snuff will help numb that too.

Even with snuff at the ready, we learned very quickly to be careful with the snakes. We always kept an eye out for them, especially the crafty black racers, though that wasn't easy to do. These lightning-fast snakes would creep up alongside you out of nowhere it seemed. They could even outrun a car. Uncle Robert would try to run them over, and if that thing wasn't hit straight on or didn't meet its end in the fan belt, he'd open the hood to find it lurking there. And as soon as that sucker would spot you, you'd better be on the run.

Today, I don't like snakes, but I'm not afraid of them. If you're from the South, you can smell them, especially the rattlesnakes. It's a smell in between a fresh pond or a fish and once you know it, you always will. The snakes are going to warn you before they do anything. You learn to accept and live with animals, any and all kinds, living like we did in the country.

Hard work, I mean the kind that makes you ache so badly that you can hardly move once you finally sit down, the kind of work you remember doing fifty years later even if you've tried to erase the memory, was as necessary for us on the farm as was feeding our animals. Picking cotton was a job like that for me. Uncle Robert and

I did that backbreaking work for many white farmers and also Mr. Basset, a neighbor a few farms over, for what seemed like eighteen or nineteen hours a day. Bending over and picking and filling the bags and bending and picking and filling them again. And again. Every part of our bodies crouched over, for hours and hours on end.

I earned three dollars, based on the amount of cotton in my bag. Uncle Robert earned nine dollars for all that work.

Oh Lord, it was horrible, picking that cotton. I never wanted to do it again. Uncle Robert had to whip my butt to get me back out in the field.

It just didn't seem right to me, that little money for that much work.

But it was right to him because he had to feed his family.

On a typical Saturday morning, Uncle Robert, Jerry, and I would get Big Red ready and go hunting or gather firewood with our big red wagon—a real honest-to-goodness red wagon that could carry 500 to 600 pounds. Sometimes it'd be so cold you could see steam coming out of Red's mouth and nostrils. Even though we had gloves on, our fingers felt like they were damn near frostbitten. Uncle Robert would take his saw and axes, and we'd carefully chop the trees at a certain angle so they'd fall how we wanted them. He'd cut the trunks into logs that we'd haul onto the wagon.

We'd fuss and cry, young boys doing work like that in the freezing cold. But it didn't matter. By the age of five or six, it was expected in this world that you'd contribute. And we needed this wood to cook with, to keep the house warm.

That's what we had to do to survive.

NEVER KNOW WHAT YOU WILL PULL OUT OF A WELL

For those of us lucky enough to have running water, you can easily take for granted being able to turn on the faucet or flush your toilet. Not so on our farm.

One of my chores was to collect our water. I'd have to pull up fifteen buckets each day from our well. I'd roll down the crank to lower the rope and bucket into the well and then wind it back up again, grabbing the rope and bucket and dropping its contents into a tub that I would lug back to the house. After living in Graham a few years, my eight-year-old self could carry a tub but couldn't quite keep it from skimming the ground.

A lot of people think a well will run dry over time, but it continues to fill up. Another thing most folks don't know about a well is that you have to keep it covered at all times. You don't know what you're going to draw out of the well—except for some of the best tasting water on record.

One morning, I filled two buckets and was cranking the third back up. I reached in and found a snake coiled up at the bottom.

I gasped and dropped the full bucket back into the well. But the weight of the bucket sent the crank turning.

Thwack. Thwack. Thwack. That crank hit me smack in the middle of my forehead as the bucket bounced along the sides of the well on its way down.

"Aaaahhhhh," I yelled out.

Thwack. Thwack.

Maybe ten times.

Then maybe fifteen times.

The same spot every time in the middle of my forehead.

"Aaaaaaaahhhhhhhhh," I continued to scream, stunned and unable to move away from the blows.

Aunt Gen came running over and grabbed me, saving me from yet another hit. Blood was gushing everywhere.

She led me, dazed, to the house.

She grabbed a gray bottle with a skull and crossbones and put some turpentine on my bleeding forehead. I scampered to the comfort of Grandma Mattie's lap.

"Oh, baby, c'mere. It gonna be all right, baby," Grandma Mattie told me. "It gonna to be all right," she soothed as she rocked me in her chair in the living room. Her fingers, knotted and tired from more than eight decades of picking and pruning and surviving and so loving I'll never forget them, caressed my head and face.

With ten children my mother had to care for, that was love and compassion I'd never had.

I still have a small dent and scar about a half-inch long on my forehead. Friends today joke that I was hit in the head when I was young, and that explains a lot.

About a week earlier, country life had given me another lesson.

I was passing our hen house, getting ready for another daily chore of fetching eggs from our twenty to thirty chickens.

Aunt Gen called me over to where she was standing, next to a frozen-scared-stiff hen.

"Juunior," she said with a slow country drawl coming from lips pursed around the snuff she was chewing.

She spat.

"Juunior, there's a snake under that chicken ass."

I was very skeptical. *How do you know that, Auntie?* I wondered.

I didn't see no snake.

But the poor petrified hen wasn't moving from her nest. Those who didn't grow up on a farm probably don't know that hens will usually jump right up when you approach them during egg gathering and get back to other business.

My aunt suspected a chicken snake—a long brown snake that looks like a rattlesnake but is mainly interested in eating eggs and rats—was the reason why.

"There a snake in here," she said calmly. "So here what I'm gonna do. Juunior," she said, then spat again, "get on this side. I'm gonna move that chicken over. Just you get outta the way."

I went over to the side of the hen, trying to figure out if there really was a snake under that chicken's ass, while she grabbed the hen then threw it off to one side and out of the way.

Sure enough, a huge brown snake—and man, this thing was long—was looking right at us with an egg in its mouth.

What happened next, I'll never forget. That small woman with a fearlessness that comes from having to protect anything and everything she owned in the world grabbed that long, old snake under its head. I think the egg busted.

She twirled its body through the air while its head remained unmoving in her hands.

Once. Twice. Around again she sent the serpent's body snapping overhead until *POP* it detached from its head and flew to the floor. She then dropped its head.

The body writhed this way and that, the damn thing probably trying to find its head.

Recovered, the hen squawked and went on her way.

Now that's bravery. Pure and simple bravery.

THERE CAN ONLY BE ONE ROOSTER

On a farm, and sometimes in life, more than one male can make for a problem.

More than one male pig and they would fight each other to be the boss hog and mate with the females. More than one rooster and they could claw and peck the other to death for the prize of fertilizing the hens.

To preserve our precious animals, we had to take care of that fighting instinct.

With being hog owners came our annual roundup. We'd wait for a litter of eight or nine hogs to hit about ten months old. At that point, they weighed between 100 to150 pounds and were starting to become dominant.

That's when Uncle Robert would decide "it was time," so he'd go down to the store twenty-five miles away and get two gray cans, one with anesthesia, the other with ointment of some sort.

"Junior," my uncle would say. "T'morrow we gonna take care of the hogs."

But Uncle Robert would try to make the best of it for them. The night before the roundup, he'd make sure the animals got the best meal of their young lives. We'd make up the tastiest possible slop with our piss and anything else we could find.

Them pigs would holler all night long. Somehow they always knew something was up. There were only two times they sounded like that: when they were getting out of the crate to be killed and when we were getting ready to take their manhood.

When it became time, Uncle Robert would tie them to the fence with a loose rope, just enough to control them. Once they got the slop, all attention was on that. With the hogs now happy, my uncle would get his two cans, two blades, and the utensils out.

Moving quietly behind the first pig as he devoured his slop, he would start gently massaging its scrotum and separating the testicles.

The pig would now be in bliss, contentedly grunting and loving how things were going for him.

Then my uncle would grab a razor blade and slice the pig quickly over the skin of the first testicle.

Shocked, the pig would be barely able to finish a squeal before my uncle would move on to the other testicle. In one quick motion, he would slice that one off too. (Once, a pig turned around, letting out a squeal like nothing I've ever heard.)

Uncle Robert would slap some ointment on the wounds and toss the testicles into a bucket.

One time, he loosened the rope and a hog flew to the mud pit, where he lay quietly the rest of the day. You could've kick that hog and it wouldn't have budged.

Without testosterone, the hogs would lose the desire to mate, would grow bigger, and their meat would be preserved and more tender and better for selling at the market. But there was one final use for the pig's manhood—in Uncle Robert's version of the Whopper sandwich. He'd boil and then fry up their testicles like Rocky Mountain oysters, slap them between some bread, and throw on some mayonnaise and have himself a huge sandwich.

What he couldn't eat, he'd throw to the hogs, who'd devour what was once a part of themselves or their littermates.

Beyond Uncle Robert's Whopper sandwich, we'd eventually use every last little part of the animal. We'd cook up the ears, tail, and feet, commonly known delicacies in the South, and make South meat out of the flesh of its head—any true Southerner will know about that meat jelly, if not tried it themselves.

With chickens, if another male entered the picture, there could be a fight to the death. The rooster had a big job. If you had, say, 200 hens, the rooster had to have his way in the biblical sense with every last one, maybe several times a day, to keep the eggs coming.

So you'd send off the ones you didn't want, or who could no longer keep up, to become dinner somewhere like a Popeye's or Kentucky Fried Chicken, and you'd replace him with a younger one.

But the hens, as long as they were producing eggs, didn't have nothin' to worry about.

The pecking order on a farm, for right or wrong, was as clear and simple as that well water.

THE SCHOOLHOUSE AND STEPHENS

After our early morning chores, Jerry and I would wait for the school bus that'd pass by our farm at five thirty a.m. Wearing overalls and a checkered shirt as all the boys did, we'd board the bus, which picked us up and any students within a ten- to fifteen-mile radius.

It dropped us off on Country Road 515 at a good ol' fashioned all-grade, one-room school. Technically, it was a room in the old Mount Carmel United Methodist Church, but we called it "The Schoolhouse."

Two teachers instructed roughly fifty students of all grades and ages. For us younger kids, we learned from the older ones and that made us faster in picking up things than students in a modern-school setting.

There was NO such thing as talking back, not at home, not to your neighbor, and never at school. That only happened in the city. If you did talk back, your teacher or cousin or whoever could whip your butt. Then your parents would beat you again because someone else had to.

I got more than an education at The Schoolhouse; that's where I also got my last name of Cooley. Jerry, who'd attended the school before I arrived, had the last name of his father, Cooley, who also fathered two other children with my mama.

When I became a student in this close-knit environment, I had no birth certificate or other official paperwork, so they decided to call me Cooley too to prevent confusion over who we were.

So I was a Stephens from my mother's side; I could claim the name Bradford from my father; and now I was a Cooley after the man who fathered several of my siblings.

Nothing about my family background—or who I was—was clear or simple.

To add to that, as I would come to realize once I was grown and away, nearly everyone in this backwoods town where the Stephenses had lived for more than a century was related in one way or another.

We'd get on the bus and at least 90 percent of the children had the last name Stephens. We'd call everyone "cousin" or "aunt" or "uncle"; it's a Southern thing, but here it's likely they were.

That's just how it was in that part of the South, where we held on to our past and to how we were living in the present with a stubbornness or blindness that sometimes left us unable to see the future.

School here wasn't mandatory, and at times we'd have to leave early to work the cotton fields or the sugar cane fields. Now the sugar cane fields I didn't mind like I did the cotton fields, especially when Grandma Mattie would cut the end of a cane and the juices so sweet and pure would run down our hands and mouths. She'd cut down the tall cane until it was a stick we'd suck until every last bit of sweetness was gone. It was better than any candy you'll ever find.

After chores, we'd change into our crisp, white button-down shirts and go back to the same church where we had been for school. This was another daily, or nearly every day, activity. Religion and our churchgoing ways were rooted in a Deep, and I mean the Deep-down, South tradition. It was standard operating procedure for those of us living in the Bible Belt.

We may not have had anything else, but we had God. Grandpa Stephens had God; he'd been a Methodist preacher. My daddy had God; he'd been a preacher too. My mama had God, most every Sunday. Even at that young age, I'd wonder—if there's no higher power, no bigger plan for us, then why do we bother to get up in the morning?

My youngest sister remarks that I can quote Scripture. I didn't just attend church and sit in the back row or show up to impress a girl or anyone else. Scripture, and my faith in our Lord and Savior, is as fundamental to me as my beating heart. I'm not just a Sunday student of the Lord.

Me in my Sunday best at seven years old (1966)

★★

On the farm, there was a closeness—with your kin, your neighbors, your surroundings— that's hard to find elsewhere. Maybe it comes from having picked the apple you're eating or the potato you're frying or killing the meat on your dinner plate.

Maybe I learned it from taking baths in the same hot water as my aunt, uncle, and grandma; there was a pecking order to that too: Uncle Robert first, then Aunt Gen, then Grandma Mattie, until by the time I got in, there was nothing but brown water.

I had a special kind of closeness with Grandma Mattie. She looked after me

Grandma Mattie in her early 70's

in ways I hadn't been used to, like when I had to go to the bathroom in the middle of the night.

When you're a child and you wake up from a deep sleep and the nearest bathroom is the outhouse hundreds of feet away in the cold or dark, you have two immediate options: Try to make it to a nearby tin can you can squat over or go on yourself.

"Baby, don't worry 'bout it," Grandma Mattie would say when the latter of the two would happen. "I'll clean you up. Lemme clean you up."

My grandmother's hands would again wipe away the pain and the piss and all the other challenges that come with childhood.

My mama was the youngest of her four kids, and out of her sixteen grandbabies, I would be the only one still around—Jerry would leave Graham before me. I was the last grandbaby to be with her before she died. And frankly, not many people paid her much attention. Maybe it was her age, but it was a good thing because I got lots of one-on-one time with her. She was my delight, and I know I was hers.

She was eightysomething years old, which sure seemed old to me, when she would rock me back and forth in her rocking chair telling me stories about her childhood and old family remedies. She knew how to soothe a burn by chanting and blowing on it. Seriously, it worked. The burning would lessen just by cupping your hands and blowing on the wound a certain way.

This great lady with long, beautiful black hair that she often wore in pigtails and with big brown eyes full of kindness left me with memories and lessons that will forever stay with me.

Once, I went outside to dig up a bucketful of worms for fishing bait. I brought it proudly into the house to show my grandma, smiling ear to ear.

"Look at what I got here, Grandma!" I said.

She looked, alright, and then said what I thought was the sweetest thing.

"Boy, boy, boy," she said, "you got yourself somethin'—a whole lot of nuthin!"

I left still smiling, remembering only the words "You got yourself . . . a whole lot . . ."

She always cheered me up and left me with a little ray of sunshine, no matter what she was actually saying.

Then there were the times she'd put me on her knee and tell me how I was special. How I had the "gift" that God had given only a few in our family of being able to see and understand things that most people can't. It's a sixth sense, an ability to communicate without words—an ability to see and *know* certain things that don't have to be physically in front of us.

"Boy, boy, boy, you are one special kid," she'd tell me. "You gonna be someone special someday. I just know it. You gonna make great things happen."

On the farm, I learned respect for elders and their wisdom and for the animals that gave us food and for the trees that gave us fruit and shade and heat. I learned about hard work, responsibility, and meeting expectations. Without those things, you weren't gonna last long on the farm.

I learned about character and most importantly faith In God , I also learned that while we weren't rich in dollars we were rich in love.

If our life's path is made up of stepping stones, then the farm was my first one. Later, I'd realize that my time there had laid the foundation I'd need to carry me to other destinations, on other journeys.

After five and a half years though, I felt a gnawing that I should rejoin my mother and my siblings. At age eleven, I was outgrowing Graham.

I decided it was time for me to return to Chattanooga and my city kin.

FAMILY TREE

There are a lot of Stephenses and offshoots of Stephenses, so to make it easier to follow my story, I've put together a family tree on my mother's side of my immediate family members. Last names listed here are the maiden and/or last names they commonly used.

My Aunt Alberta and Aunt Geneva in their early 20's

Grandfather Robert Stephens—born around 1840 (a former slave and landowner who had twenty-one children)

Grandmother Mattie Blake—born December 10, 1889

Uncle Buster—born 1919

Aunt Beatrice (Bert)—born 1921

Aunt Geneva (Gen)—born 1923

My mother, Gladys Stephens—born 1927

My mother's children:

Mary (also known as Doll) Stephens—born 1941

Rosemary (Rose) Stephens—born 1943

Joe (also known as Snug) Askew—born 1946

Robert (also known as PeeWee) Cooley—born 1955

Will (Willie) Cooley—born 1957

Jerry Cooley—born 1958

James (Bradford) Cooley—born 1959

Gaylo Jo (Gail) Holloway-Sutton—born 1961

Joey (also known as Chubby) Holloway—born 1963

Jonathan (also known as Nathan) Holloway—born 1964

I was born in the middle of two sets of siblings who came from the same father. I was perhaps the black sheep of the family, or at least my mother was always afraid of that, so she kept a watchful eye on me. She also loved my father deeply. I think that's why I was the only one of her male children she called Junior, even though several others also had the same first name as their father.

PART II:
THE CITY

I'd adopted the look and language of Southern country life, and my classmates didn't let me forget it.

—**upon my return to the city**

COUNTRY BOY, CITY BOY

As I'd asked, my mama and her boyfriend, Joe Holloway, visited the farm to fetch and take me back home. When I got back, I quickly realized that I may have returned to my roots but things weren't the same.

I'd returned wearing overalls and a checkered shirt while my sister Gail remembers that they wore "regular" clothes, whatever those were. I had the strong Southern drawl of the deep woods. I said po' instead of poor, y'all instead of just you. I'd adopted the look and language of Southern country life, and my classmates didn't let me forget it.

The first couple of years back were tough because I was different and they treated me that way. My classmates called me "country" and I called them "city" to retaliate.

As it turned out, I had learned a lot in Graham. I was going into the fifth grade in Chattanooga but was more advanced than the others in my class at Calvin Donaldson Elementary School. They would stumble along in their reading, and I would pick up a passage and whip right through it.

Our school principal, Mr. White, would brag, "That James Cooley, he's reading on the grade level!" Meanwhile, the other students were two or three grade levels behind.

Despite Mr. White's praise, I just wanted them to accept me as "city."

I don't know if Mr. White's still living, but I hope he knows that by him saying I was reading on grade level when Darrell and George and others in class were doing third-grade reading, he had me standing on a ten-foot pole.

That success started because of the old-school Schoolhouse education I got in Alabama, where I'd had plenty of attention and older students to help prepare me. In the projects, academics were just not that important. What your mama taught you was to make sure you came home at night.

Looking back, I guess I've always been a decent student and that also goes back to the fifth grade and reading at grade level. I never fell behind academically when I got back from Alabama; I never lost that competitiveness.

I realize now that my experiences in Alabama had set that foundation and I'd never lost it, but I didn't know I'd gained it.

Over time, I heard "country boy" less and less, or maybe I just got more used to them making fun of me—except for one day when Gregory Crom called me that for the last time. I'd had it. So I lunged right into him and beat him until snot ran out of his nose. After that, I had no more problems from him.

Eventually, the name-calling stopped, and I went back to being "Junior."

Country boy though—that name showed me how I'd changed. And after a while I even became proud of the name.

My fourth grade picture upon my return to Chattanooga, Tennessee (1970)

But some things hadn't changed.

I was back in the exact same environment where gangs and crews were hanging out and people would get shot right in front of you. I still lived in one room with four of my brothers. My mama still struggled to make ends meet and had her three youngest children, now older themselves, to care for.

One day, I was getting ready for school and going through our closet upstairs to find some clean clothes to put on. There were plenty of clothes alright, both dirty and clean and piled high on the floor. Underneath them had also been rats and mice.

We were poor—dirt poor—with too many people and too much going on in our home, so that was normal for us.

I eventually found some clean underwear at the very bottom of the pile, but the rats or mice had found this pair and chewed it all up; I mean eaten that sucker up to where almost nothing remained but the elastic rubber band at the top and a few little scraps of material.

Mama gave me a forewarning before I left. "Boy, don't you wear them underwear!"

Of course, I wore them.

That very day when my bare butt happened to be showing through my underwear, me and my friends—Charles (or D'Man), who is one of my best friends to this day, Norman, who is also still my good friend, George Green, Darrel Bond, and a couple of others—decided to cut class.

Principal White caught us in the library.

He marched us into the office. I knew he was getting ready to whip our asses, but the only thing I was thinking was, *Oh Lord, my mama told me not to wear that underwear.*

At that time, school principals could punish you with a paddle with holes cut out of it to give your behind an extra sting.

And of course, I was first up.

"Drop your drawers!" Mr. White instructed.

Slowly, I did as I was told.

The others in my crew, now sitting behind me, busted out laughing.

My face burned. *God dang it!* I thought. *My mama* told *me not to wear that underwear.*

I looked back at my "friends," and they weren't worried about getting any whoppin'. They were too busy laughing at my Swiss-cheese-like underwear.

"HEY. You guys, stop!" Mr. White commanded.

But I looked up at Mr. White, and I knew he wanted to laugh too. In fact, I think I got fewer licks than the rest of them because he wanted me to pull up my drawers.

It was horrible. I never wanted to go to school again.

Norman and D'Man have never let me live that down.

There was a reason my mama told me not to wear that holey underwear.

THAT WHITE WOMAN DONE LOST HER MIND

The next stop after elementary school for those of us in the Alton Park projects, where my family now lived, was Alton Park Junior High. Norman, D'Man, and I entered seventh grade together, and we met Billy Harper in the eighth grade. Billy and I forged a bond that has lasted to this day.

We were goofy teenagers and I became known there, just as I was known in my home and neighborhood, for having an outgoing personality. I'd crack a joke in a minute. Though I'd act the fool, I was apparently a good student.

We had one white teacher in the entire school. Her name escapes me now, though I've tried and tried to remember it, but I can picture her clearly and hear her words that sent me on an entirely different path, just like when I was six and went to the farm in Alabama.

She was maybe twenty-eight, a very pretty blonde. She had high expectations, and you knew it.

With me, she'd always wink my way during class. She was trying, in a positive way, to keep my attention directed on the work and not on telling the next joke.

I remember awards day in seventh grade. We were all in the auditorium, probably 400 kids. We had some smart kids, and I was not one of them. Paula Harris, the smarty-pants who always won everything, was going to win again. We all knew it.

I never thought I was going to win anything at all. I was wrong.

This teacher called me up to give me the best-science-student award, saying "I'd like to point this student out. He's very smart, very bright and has shown me he has the potential to be a leader in the world. I believe that one day he will be."

I was shocked. I couldn't believe I had won this award, much less what she was saying.

I still have the little trophy today.

As we were nearing the end of ninth grade, the last year of junior high school in Chattanooga, she approached me near the lockers after class got out.

She asked me if I was going to be attending Howard High School, the school right up the street that drew from my neighborhood, or if I was thinking about Kirkman Technical.

Now Kirkman was seven or eight miles across the city. It wasn't in my neighborhood zone, and I had no way to get there. It was also a specialized vocational school that you had to pass a test to get into. It was one of the top schools in the city and one of only four vocational schools in the state. I wasn't smart enough to get in. No way.

There was no way was I going to Kirkman Technical.

"I've been watching you over these last three years," she said. "You cannot follow your brothers and sisters to Howard. You're better than that. You're smarter than that. You're going to be something someday. You're smarter than these kids."

I looked at her, practically dumbfounded.

What's wrong with this crazy white woman? I thought.

Even though I was the class clown, she probably saw through that.

"I have become very fond of you over these years. I've learned to love you. You're better than that."

Now my jaw really dropped. I could not believe it, that word she said.

Love.

That word was never actually spoken in my world. Sure, you knew you loved your sisters and brothers and parents and grandparents. You knew it. You just never said it.

But this white woman teaching in the ghetto was the first person who said the word love aloud to me. The very first person.

This white woman done lost her mind, I thought. That must be it. That would explain what she said.

Done. Lost. Her. Mind.

Well, despite what she said, I still had to take the test and find a way to get to the school if I got in.

"Suppose I talk to your mom or dad or whoever and get you set up to take the test?" she asked.

She thinks I can pass the test? I'm not gonna pass. I'm still going to Howard, I told myself. *But okay, I'll take the stupid test.*

I took the test and passed.

As it so happened, Billy, who lived in the Kirkman zone even though he attended Alton Park Junior High, and Norman, who had recently moved to the Kirkman zone, would also be going to that high school.

I don't think I ever thanked that teacher, and now I can't remember her name. Billy, Norman, and I have racked our brains all these years later to try and piece that part of our lives back together.

That's another lesson I learned: Show your love and appreciation when it's still fresh, while you still can.

This former country boy enrolled in one of the best high schools in the city, but now I had to figure out how to get there. It was a challenge, because the only students from Alton Park to attend Kirkman were me and three girls.

Everyone knew each other in the 'hood where I lived, but this school was in downtown Chattanooga. If you worked for the city or electric company, you would be close by. Of if you were in the fancy neighborhoods of Hixson or Lookout Mountain, in the heart of the city where the upper-class whites who ran the city lived, you could get there easily enough.

There was a clear divide at that time in this city set along the Tennessee River in the foothills of the Appalachian Mountains. Four quadrants separated the population into four levels of prosperity and races. The upper- and middle-class Negroes stayed in the south and west parts, while the poor white folks stayed in the north and east. Poor black people like me and my family stayed in Alton Park and surrounding neighborhoods in the southern part of the city. There was just one white family in our project, and if you weren't from there, we knew it.

Thinking back, it seems like these racial divides were part of a design to keep some of the population—like those of us in the projects—in their areas. In fact, the government practically made sure that would happen by providing you everything you needed like a subsidized home with electricity and water and food, as they did with my family. It was just enough to keep us alive but certainly not enough to help us move to the better side of town.

Most of the time, I ended up thumbing a ride to school, which despite the danger in my neighborhood, was common practice.

Norman, my oldest friend since elementary school, Billy, my very best friend to this day, Ernest, Norman's first cousin who I met in tenth grade when he came down from Chicago, and I formed a tight core group almost immediately at Kirkman.

We were always involved in something, especially sports. Norman still chuckles when he thinks of how I'd make members of the other team laugh when we'd play basketball. I was a jokester, just as in junior high.

Our shop teacher, Mr. Stephens—not related—got the brunt of that. Norman, Billy, and I were in his class together, as we were in many others, for two years. We'd crack jokes when he'd turn to write on the chalkboard or, really, at any opportunity. He liked me and even gave me a job through a program to help underprivileged students, but I eventually wore on him until one day he said, "James Cooley, you've been cracking all these jokes. So I've got one for you. Two elephants bumped asses, and guess what came out? You!"

I had another side though: I was determined and driven to win. So while I'd make the other team laugh on the basketball court, I hated to lose to them.

That's maybe why I was voted "Most Likely to Succeed" along with "Class Clown." In fact, I was even included twice in the *Who's Who of American High School Students*. I'm not quite sure why because I didn't have the greatest grades, but I think it had something to do with leadership.

In twelfth grade, our group expanded to about a dozen boys and we gave ourselves a name: The Players Club. We were popular, and we knew it. We had T-shirts made up that proudly displayed "The Players Club" on them, and we had our own table in the cafeteria. We were even allowed to rope it off. You could only eat with us if Norman, Billy, or I authorized you to enter.

We had no trouble inviting in the girls though.

We walked around in our Players Club T-shirts and big afros. Ernest and Norman had the biggest 'fros out of the entire school, just like Don Cornelius on *Soul Train*. It was 1976 and '77, after all, at the height of big hair and bell bottoms.

Billy was voted "Most Handsome" and "Best Dressed." He was also the quarterback on the football team and always had the most beautiful girls in school wanting to be his girlfriends.

I was "Coolman" to Billy, and we made sure we were in the best position to meet these girls.

For two semesters we took tailoring, which had thirty-five girls and me and Billy in the class. We thought we were going to make our own suits and look all fancy, but we ended up just talking about what girls we wanted to get together with.

We just could not concentrate. I think I only learned how to make a pocket and hem up some pants.

The Players Club. We thought we were so cool, and maybe we were back then, but I sit back now and think about how silly we were and just shake my head. So many things that we thought were important at the time—like having the best-looking girlfriend or the best table at lunch—so much of that you leave behind the day you graduate.

NOBODY'S BABY DADDY

Even with our girl-crazed teenage antics, I was able to avoid other pressures that came with my age and circumstances. I never stole or became a gang member or a drug addict, even though all of that surrounded me once I returned home at night to the projects. Seeing that happen in the neighbor's home, in the groups hanging out on the street corners, in your own home with your siblings and their friends, it was nearly impossible not to go down that path.

To be true, I did experiment. After school, my boys and I would go over to my sister Doll's apartment in public housing and drink cans of Schlitz Malt Liquor or Wild Irish Rose fortified wine. I can't even tell you how stupid drunk we got at our senior prom off that cheap booze.

I avoided becoming a statistic in part because of that teacher in ninth grade, one of the first times a person recognized me for having potential in school. *I can do this. I can be successful if given an opportunity*, I kept telling myself. I did not want to let her down

The Bethlehem Center, a recreational center where we could gather and shoot hoops or play hopscotch and let off steam, also helped steer me in a better direction. We neighborhood kids called it "The Beth." It was a positive outlet that diverted our attention from what was happening all around us.

These things helped me break what I call a generational curse that I saw even then but didn't fully grasp the pull of until later.

There was almost no way out of the projects except for death if you were a man or by having babies if you were a woman.

If you lived to graduate from high school you had made it, not that anyone was encouraged to go to school. As a girl, if you made it beyond fifteen or sixteen without getting pregnant, you were in good hands.

And guys thought it was cool to get a girl pregnant. No one was married or thinking about marriage. The expectation just was not there.

We had a name for guys like that: your mama's baby daddy. I listen to a lot of women today who think it's cool to say, "That's my baby daddy." Every time I hear that term, it drives me crazy.

For me, I never wanted to be called someone's baby daddy because my daddy *was* my mama's baby daddy. It's painful to say that even years later, but it's true.

I made it a point that I was not going to get anyone pregnant, not unless I was married.

A sign for Alton Park (Spencer J. McCallie homes) that illustrates there is no way out and no path for success. I proved that wrong.

After all, I saw firsthand what that would lead to. I felt the sharp pangs of being on the outside looking in on an intact family. I saw my mother raise ten kids from six daddies. I saw my oldest sister, Doll, get pregnant at sixteen or seventeen, and the same thing happen with Rose, the next sibling after her. In The Players Club, several friends who I won't name didn't make it out unscathed and another one very nearly didn't. I don't think I know of any girl who was African-American who made it out of my neighborhood or high school without getting pregnant.

I wanted to break free from the generational curse, from the cycle that was happening over and over as behaviors and ways of life were passed along from granddaddies or grandmas to fathers or mothers and then to their sons or daughters.

The only way to put a stop to that curse and create a gap in the cycle is to leave that toxic environment or find a way to get a new vision so you can see a different path. That other path for me had been Alabama.

Still, why so many babies? Why so many baby daddies? My sister Doll used to ask my mama those questions.

Doll says she never dreamed of having five kids, much less ten like Mama had. She used to ask her, "How in the world did you have ten kids, Mama?"

My mama told her that she didn't really know. That it was just something that happened. That God put us on this earth, and we had to replenish this earth.

And why did my family think it was okay, as I was to find out later, to have babies with kinfolk? (That's a whole 'nother story that I'm still grappling with.)

Maybe it's rural life. Maybe it's Southern life. Maybe it's life in the 'hood. Or maybe it's all three. But it's still real in the black community today.

What I do know is how I felt as an illegitimate kid—like an outsider.

I swore to myself that my children would always know their father. I would always be there regardless of what they or I were going through.

A STEAK CUT RIGHT DOWN THE MIDDLE

Here is what I know about my father, the Reverend James Bradford: He was a preacher, but I didn't recall at which church until I came across his obituary recently.

He had four children from his first wife, Joyce, and five stepchildren from his second, Ms. Shirley.

I saw him as a child, but I don't recall how many times. Maybe it was ten times or fifteen, max.

I look like him.

I look *just* like his third son, Michael, who was born two months after me.

Because of that, there was no way to deny me, no matter how quiet things had been kept about who James Bradford had fathered.

My father did acknowledge me in private, like around my mama and my sisters and brothers. He married Ms. Shirley after I returned from Alabama, and she got wind of my holey underwear and made him take me shopping so I would at least have the basics. The three or four times she made him do this, he'd send me back home with a few packets of underwear. It was known that he was my father, it just wasn't talked about.

Not even in his obituary.

After he died at the age of forty-five of a massive heart attack on the biggest day of his Christian life—just before he was to preach his trial sermon at the New Enon Baptist Church—his obituary listed his survivors. It names his four children; it names his wife, Shirley, and his five stepchildren; it lists his mother and stepfather; his sisters and his brothers.

It does not include me.

My father, I'm told, was a very profound speaker. His church community called him "Big Jim Bradford."

When he died, the church was packed, waiting for him to deliver his sermon. Doll was there that day and rushed to call me. "Junior," she said, "have you heard?" I wasn't in church but felt like I should have been. "Your dad just died."

I was fifteen, in ninth grade, and I played it off like it was no big deal. I loosely knew a couple of my half-brothers and stepbrothers through school but had no real relationship with them. No one at school said anything to me, at least not to my face, about being one of James Bradford's sons, and I didn't say anything about it either. I told myself I didn't care, that it didn't affect me and even if it did, I wouldn't let it. I didn't go to the funeral and don't remember really wanting to. My father just wasn't in my life like that.

That haunted me for years afterward.

For the next four of five years, I'd drive by the home of my father's first wife and my half-brothers and half-sister. Now that he was gone, I wanted to show myself to this side of my family and introduce myself to Joyce, who I had not met before.

One night, I was on leave from the Navy and drove by the house. On this particular night, I finally told myself I was tired of this. I stopped the car about six p.m. and got up enough nerve to walk up the yard and knock on the door. Joyce answered.

I didn't have to tell her who I was. "You are James's son," she said. "I always knew this day would come. Come on in. We're eating dinner."

All four of my half-siblings were at the table eating. My half-sister Darlene looked at me and then looked at Michael.

"Mommy, him and Michael look just alike," she said.

"They do favor each other a lot," Joyce replied. "Now go ahead and eat."

I and my half-brother Ronnie put our forks on the steak at the same time. We paused and looked at it and each other. Joyce picked up a knife and cut the steak right down the middle.

PART III

THE NAVY

"My parting wish for you men and women of my detachment is that you will place your faith [in the Lord], develop your personal vision of the world, and see life not as it is but how it should be."

—message to my sailors the Change of Command Ceremony at US Naval Air Facility, Misawa, Japan

WELCOME TO THE NAVY

For twenty-three years, one month, and twenty-two days, I was a proud member of the United States Navy. I deeply believed in serving my country. I learned so much about service and sacrifice, persistence and politics, and honor, courage, and commitment. (The last part is the Navy motto, and I still live out those core values today.)

That's twenty-three years of highs and lows, of working with thousands of sailors and hundreds of commanders as I rose through the ranks to become a commissioned officer.

For this book that's intended to be a snapshot of my life's journeys, I can only touch on the high points of this career that took me around the globe and eventually to the White House.

Here's how it started:

In June 1978, I graduated from Kirkman Technical High School. I had successfully grown up in the projects and made it through high school, which was a major accomplishment in itself.

But as for what happened after that, there was only one road that led to employment for someone uneducated or only having a high school diploma in my world.

You could work at Little Debbie, which made those Swiss Rolls and Oatmeal Cream Pies and other little cakes, or stretch yarn used to make carpets in one of the yarn factories around Chattanooga and the Georgia state line; or you could work in the local chicken house where you'd help slaughter some 1,000 birds a day and come home covered in chicken poop.

I knew where the path was going to lead for a young man like me. It wasn't gonna change. I was going to work at Little Debbie, the yarn factory, the chicken house, or at some other job that would only take me so far in life. And it wasn't going to be far.

For that summer after high school, I did work for the yarn factory making five dollars an hour—decent money, I thought.

But one day in early September, I saw a "Navy" sign as I rode the bus near downtown. Me and my boys in high school had talked about the military. My best friend, Billy Harper, and I had even discussed going into the service on the buddy-buddy plan, only to see that plan be pushed aside when he suffered a serious knee injury during a football game. When I spotted the Navy sign that day, for some reason I had a paradigm shift.

I already knew what I was going to get walking down the path I was on. So like that poem of Robert Frost's about taking the path less traveled, I decided to take the one no one else was on.

One of the biggest challenges for most of us is having the confidence and courage to do something no one else is doing. I turned and went left instead of right that day and jumped on a bus and rode it down a new road. That's an analogy, but there's also a lot of truth in it for me.

I stopped at that Navy sign and enlisted and literally jumped on that bus.

On September 10, 1978, I left Chattanooga for Knoxville, Tennessee, where I was sworn in and put on a plane to Orlando, Florida, for boot camp. I'd never been on a plane before. The farthest I'd been from home was to Disney World in Orlando for a high school senior trip. My whole world had been a three- to five-mile radius in Chattanooga.

We arrived about one a.m. on September 11, eighty-nine of us new Navy recruits, some with long hair, some hippies, all of us looking at one other, and no one saying anything.

We went to our bunks and were able to lie down for an hour and a half until about two thirty a.m. when this crazy guy in his uniform (actually a company commander, but at two thirty a.m., anyone will look like a crazy guy) came in and threw a garbage can down with a tremendous force.

BOOM!

The reverberation from the hollow steel can bolted us awake.

"HEY! YOU. GET UP!" he screamed as loud as he could. He stormed around the room, getting right in our faces.

"YOU! What in the hell are you doing in here sleeping! You're now officially in the United States of America Navy," he hollered. "GET UP! Grab your stuff!"

We had lots of different personalities among us, guys from New York, New Jersey, the Midwest, and the South like me, and you could tell who had gold teeth and was going to try and be a badass. Me, I was a country boy at heart and aside from making jokes was never a real troublemaker, so I just sat back quietly and listened.

This company commander was breathing in our faces, and all I was thinking was, *Oh Lord, what have I gotten myself into?*, not knowing that this was the start of a brand-new life and an attitude adjustment.

Why did I leave Chattanooga for all of this? To come to this and get screamed at? I thought.

A bit later that day, we marched to the barber shop to have our heads shaved. Everyone—long-haired, with big afros, already-short hair, no matter what—got the same haircut. It was all going to be cut off.

We were then marched to breakfast, where we learned we had to be close. And I mean bumping into each other, crotch-to-butt close. We also learned we would only have fifteen minutes to eat. That time wasn't just for you but for your entire company. If you were in the back of the line, you might not get to eat that day but for one or two minutes because so many other units had to get in and eat after you.

Then we had to get our uniforms. Navy sailors wear dungarees, kind of like a prison outfit with a blue shirt, jeans, or loose pants. We stenciled our names on the back of our pants and the front of our jerseys.

All of this set the tone for uniformity and how we would be expected to function as a unit. All eighty-eight or ninety-two of the guys in your unit had to become one because when you're fighting out there you don't have time for divisions. This is real. You've got bullets flying out there for real. You've got to learn to love your brother and protect them and rely on them to do the same, no matter where you or he came from.

Our indoctrination into the Navy was underway, but a big problem loomed as I got into boot camp: the swim test.

Before you were even locked into a company, you had to be able to float for five minutes and swim a lap, among other physical fitness tests you had to pass.

Most of the white guys jumped right in and floated and swam and passed. Not so with the brothers, the 200 of us who were African-American. To be honest, and there are always exceptions to the rule, we just weren't taught to swim. At least not from what I had seen.

For me, I just could not get it, though I tried and tried to relax and not panic in the water.

Now if you couldn't get it within fourteen days, you would be processed out of the Navy and sent back home. I was down to my very last day, and it happened to be on my birthday, September 25—my birthday, the day I was either gonna learn how to swim or sink. It was my last day, my last chance.

For some reason, I jumped into the outdoor Olympic-sized pool, rolled over onto my back, and—suddenly I was floating! For about three minutes, I kept calm and remained on my back. But then I started to panic. However, it had been a cloudy day and it started pouring down on us just when I had two minutes to go. For some reason the Lord was with me because if it hadn't started raining, I would have gone home for sure.

The company commander told me to get out and go over to where they would put me in my company. Welcome to the Navy, he told me.

I was behind two weeks in boot camp because of my inability to swim, but that incident gave me confidence that if I could overcome that hurdle, I could do almost anything.

The company commander, Chief Petty Officer Evans, who I was now assigned to, looked through our Armed Services Vocational Aptitude Battery (ASVAB) tests and records. He didn't choose me for a leadership role at first; I was just one of the members of his company. But that changed before long.

Our company was so bad at marching and drilling that we became known as the "marching misfits." It even became our company slogan that we put on our flag and carried around to represent us.

I was marching in the back one day when the company commander ran back and called out, "Column left, march!" I was marching pretty tight I guess and had caught his eye. He kept watching me and said, "Hey! Do that again, boy. Column left, march!"

I was so happy to be noticed that I marched even better, summoning up every ounce of energy I had, keeping my head straight and my eyes forward.

In a marching formation, everything operates off the right-wing guide. The company follows your lead and timing. The commander grabbed me by the arm and said I was going be the right-wing guide. I was going be *the* guy the whole company marched off from here on out. They were going to be following *my* lead.

As a drill instructor/Navy company commander at the recruit training command in Great Lakes, Illinois (1990)

This gave me extreme self-confidence, and at that point I told myself I was going to be a company commander someday. And when I became a first class petty officer a few years later, I did become a company commander—a Navy drill instructor. That's considered special duty, and most sailors don't get the opportunity to get a special duty, like recruiting or being a drill instructor. It takes a certain kind of person to do those jobs.

For me, earning that position fulfilled a dream I'd had back in boot camp in 1978.

POINTS OF LIGHT

Following boot camp, I elected to go to Radioman "A" School in San Diego, California. I was able to use the three years that I had studied electronics and technology at Kirkman Technical High School to land a spot in one of the most sought out posts in the service.

From there, I was assigned to the USS *Barney* in Norfolk, Virginia. A light of good fortune shined my way when I met Dan Goodwin. He was a second class petty officer and a sharp radioman. I sure looked up to this guy, and he took me under his wing. He was well-respected otherwise, which was a good thing because my leading petty officer, or LPO, wasn't fond of me. The LPO didn't think I understood the flow of radio traffic and radio patching and definitely did not think I was very smart. He had been in sixteen years and was a first class petty officer, so this was a serious issue. He didn't think I could catch on and tried to get rid of me.

But Dan wouldn't let him. He kept telling him I would be okay, and he kept teaching me the ropes of the technical side of IT and how to be a future leader in the Navy. Dan eventually got promoted to first class petty officer while the LPO got in trouble for losing crypto material—top secret material that would allow an enemy to decrypt radio traffic and communication if they got ahold of it. He was demoted and eventually retired at the rank of second-class petty officer.

I was on the *Barney* for eighteen months before I fell ill and was diagnosed with thyroid cancer, the same disease my mama had suffered from years earlier. I did not know it was going to be hereditary. Doctors discovered my cancer when I went in for medical clearance. They quickly pulled me off the ship and gave me a dose of radioactive iodine. When that showed no results, I was given a second dose, which completely killed my thyroid gland. For the next two years, I was on shore duty until I reenlisted and got orders for the Naval Communication Station in Exmouth, Australia.

I was assigned to the tech control division in Exmouth. Thanks to Dan the Radioman, I was extremely technical and able to prove that to the command staff there. I also had the good fortune of having another supervisor, Rudy Paisley, there who was one of the best tech controllers I have ever worked with. He showed me the technical ropes, and more.

The first person I met when I checked on board in Exmouth was Charles Stewart. He was ten years older than me. We clicked right away. He and my supervisor Rudy and I shared a love of sports. We played rugby, basketball, and football on a competitive level. We played on the US pro basketball team in Australia and amassed winning records in the other sports too.

Charles and I became inseparable. He was just as competitive in life as he was in sports, and he kept pushing me in Exmouth and beyond as our careers took us to the Bay Area and other stations. He pushed me to go to college and then pushed me to go to graduate school and become an officer. And I did the same with him.

He was like a big brother to me.

Our careers remained intertwined even when my officer's duties took me to the Pentagon and then on to work in the White House.

Charles was stationed at other assignments, but I was only a phone call away.

I had another mentor waiting to pick up where Charles Stewart left off when I arrived in Guam, at that time one of four Navy NAVCAMs, which are now called Naval Computer and Telecommunications Area Master Stations. Chuck May, the Naval Criminal Investigative Service (NCIS) special agent for the base and an Army captain, was there to make sure my light would continue to shine.

Chuck was also an athlete and quickly befriended me, an E-6 moving up the enlisted ranks but certainly not yet at the top. He asked, "Why don't you play basketball with us on the officers' team?" I jumped at that offer. I also used to play one-on-one with him. He was as much an athlete as I was, maybe more so, and was just as competitive, and he'd beat the hell out of me on a regular basis. This frustrated me to no end, until one day I figured out how to beat him. I thought I had won the lotto.

Chuck had played football for George Mason University in Virginia. A star running back, he got drafted to play pro but chose instead to play in the now-defunct United States Football League and the Canadian Football League. In Australia, I had played basketball and rugby on a nearly professional level, so I was no benchwarmer myself. At Exmouth, I had become the best athlete and led the league in scoring in two of my three seasons on our base varsity teams. We competed against and beat many of the professional teams there.

Still, I would say that Chuck taught me the real meaning of drive. He used to tell me, "Me and you are just alike. Whether you know it or not, the only thing different between me and you is I'm already successful because I've gone to college and have chosen a career field that I love."

Over time, that seeped in. He would teach law enforcement on the nearby islands of Pohnpei and Saipan and would take me with him to teach command fitness training. In turn, he taught me what leadership is about.

"One day, you're going be more successful than me," he'd tell me. "You're going be an officer one day. Always remember, you are James Cooley. Just do things your way. Everyone will adjust."

Chuck went on to be selected as a one-star Army general. While I initially dismissed what he was telling me, I did become an officer. And he is one of the reasons why. His drive fueled my own.

In my first evaluation at Great Lakes, I ranked seventy out of more than 400 company commanders. I was pissed. For someone who had amassed a record like mine, that was like a smack across the face. I could not believe my ranking and did not think it was fair.

I talked to the commanding officer about it, and he replied, "Well, Chief Cooley, I can see you making senior chief. But I don't think you've got officer potential."

After some back and forth, he moved me up about ten spots to sixty, but again he told me he didn't think I was officer material. "You'll make senior chief, but that's probably as far as you'll go," he said.

Oh, I'll show you, I thought.

The next thing I knew I was the top drill instructor on base. Then I became a master training specialist and a curriculum development instructor. Then some two-and-a-half years later on the USS *Blue Ridge*, I became a commissioned officer.

I called this commander up one day.

"Sir, remember that day you told me I was never going to be an officer? Sir, I can assure you today that I am."

He said "I knew it," without hesitation.

"Sir, you told me I was only going to make senior chief—"

"Oh, I've been following your career," he interrupted. "I know what you've been doing. I always knew you were going to be an officer." He went on, "Don't you remember I pulled you up ten spots?"

Huh. He did that on purpose, I realized.

Despite some "lucky" breaks and high points in my Navy career, I did fail a whole lot in the beginning. That was a good thing. You can only experience success with failure; it's kind of like teaching your kids to be careful. You would not let them fall off a skyscraper or from a roof, but you might let them fall from their bed so they can learn how to get back up and be safe the next time. Fortunately, I had mentors who showed me what success looks like.

All of us have lights around us like those men I encountered in the Navy—but you must be able to see them. You cannot be around anyone who does not light the flame inside of you; there just isn't time. You have to surround yourself with people you can learn and grow from.

These mentors showed me that, and I thank the Lord for sending me their light.

LEADING BY EXAMPLE

Along with becoming a drill instructor at Great Lakes, I also became certified as a career counselor. I remember speaking to a group of young sailors one day and telling them about the importance of education.

At that time, I had not yet completed my college degree. During my talk, one young man spoke up and said, "Sir, that's great. Where did you graduate from?"

I looked at him and had to answer, "Well, uh, I'm still working on it."

Don't you know that room went quiet.

That was an integrity problem right there. How could I be telling them to do something that I had not done myself? At that point, it dawned on me—if you have not been through the situation or circumstance, how can you come up with a solution to solve a problem or explain what constitutes success?

I remember that day extremely well. That pushed me to jump back into school and finish up my degree.

I went on to earn a degree in vocational education studies as well as a degree in training, education, and development from Southern

Illinois University in 1992. I earned a master's in public administration from Central Michigan University a few years later. Since then I have acquired an executive MBA master's certificate from the University of Notre Dame and several master's certificates from Villanova University. Today I study at Concordia University where I am working on my doctorate in education and transformational leadership.

For a boy coming from the backwoods of Alabama and the projects in Tennessee, that's not so bad.

I checked in on the USS *Blue Ridge* in Yokosuka, Japan, in 1992. All chief petty officers and above had to meet one-on-one with the commanding officer, who at the time was Captain Joy.

"What are your plans here?" he asked.

"Well, who is your number one chief? You're looking at him," I replied.

He started laughing at me.

In the Navy, there are only two amphibious command and control ships: the USS *Mount Whitney* and the USS *Blue Ridge*. The *Blue Ridge* controls all the Seventh Fleet ships from San Diego up into Yokosuka, Japan. Coming from Illinois, I had not been to sea in several years so when I came aboard the *Blue Ridge*, folks asked why I wanted to take on the number one command in the Navy.

Because the leadership possibilities were huge, and I felt ready to tackle them.

On that ship, you get orders directly from the leading commanders at the highest levels in our government and you are in charge of direct communication to and from the White House. I would be the guy responsible for making sure connectivity was there. That meant when someone picked up the phone, what we call the "red phone," to call the White House or State Department, I had to make sure it worked the first time, no matter what was going on. And if someone was picking up the red phone, something major was happening.

I was the leading chief petty officer in charge of some 165 sailors. That role changed, however, when the captain had to place new officers coming out of the Naval Academy. He didn't want a new officer running the crypto program. He called me into his office.

"Chief, I know you're not going to like this, but I'm going to take your leadership position and make you in charge of the crypto program."

"Uh, sir, but I like being in a leadership role," I said. "I've got 165 folks, and . . ." I trailed off.

Of course, he took that position away. But that meant I would be calling the shots for how the entire Seventh Fleet would protect information and prevent an enemy from decoding what we were saying or sending back and forth.

The captain had that much faith and confidence in me, because if I messed up, he was going to get fired and potentially be court-martialed.

I didn't let him down. Eight months after I arrived on board the *Blue Ridge*, I was selected to be an officer via the Limited Duty Officer Program.

"Sir, I told you when I first met you that you were looking at your number one chief," I reminded the commander after I received my commission. "And I told you I was only going to be at your command one year."

I ran these different programs at my duty stations, plus I also created the first at-sea Navy physical fitness program, which I will talk about in the next chapter.

But I also had something called conviction, which is probably why I earned the name "Do the Right Thing James Cooley." That's what the leadership team on board called me.

If something wasn't right, I wasn't going do it. The ideas of honesty, integrity, and ethics (or HIE, as I call these highly important qualities) I took seriously.

I may make mistakes and do some stupid or crazy things at times—we all do—but when it comes down to having honesty, integrity, and ethics, that's what I live by.

Being awarded a Navy commendation medal by Captain Albert Heisig for developing the Navy physical fitness readiness program

Receiving my Navy surface warfare designation (one of the fastest ever done on the USS Blueridge) from Captain Heisig

COMMANDER, YOU'RE ON THE FAT BOY PROGRAM

You know if you're a closet eater. You know deep down about your stash of Cokes and cookies and chips and crackers. I had to tell that to a Navy commander one day.

When I was stationed at Moffett Field in the San Francisco Bay Area after returning from Australia, I started to feel that I had some ability to influence others. One of our commanders was a heavyset young woman. I had been an athlete and done some fitness programs at my previous duty station. Knowing that, one day she approached me.

"Petty Officer Cooley, what can I do to lose weight?" she asked me.

It took me aback that the boss, the commander who was fifteen paygrades higher than me, had asked me such a question. I took my time in responding, finally saying, "A lot of times, we just have to be aware of what we're doing and be honest with ourselves. One of the biggest reasons people don't lose weight is because they're closet eaters."

She nodded. The next day, she brought in about four bags of chips and cookies, candy and Twinkies.

"Okay. I'm a closet eater," she said, a bit tearfully. "I just pulled out all the snacks! You were right!"

One of the things I stress to our youths and even adults is that you have to know yourself, accept yourself, and love yourself before you can share yourself with others or make any real changes.

This commander had once definitely *not* known herself or been able to admit all that she had in her pantry. Only once you're able to do that can you lose that weight and make the changes that you want. You must always be true to who you are and develop the right attitude to stay on course to meet your goals.

When I transferred to Guam, I was promoted to first class petty officer. As I had been into fitness, the commanding officer gave me the fitness coordinator position and allowed me to build out the physical readiness program, or what the Navy calls PRT, for the base.

One day, my lieutenant came in to be measured as required. Now she was my boss and she let me know it, but she was also over the body fat standards and I let her know that. I put her on PRT, or the "fat boy program" as it became known, where she would have to work out several days a week. I didn't discriminate. She got mad at me and left in a huff. But she did allow me to continue to do my job and supported me throughout my assignment in Guam.

Then a new commanding officer, a Navy captain, came to my office to be measured.

He was trying to sweet talk me while holding it all in. "Oh, Petty Officer Cooley, I've heard great things about you," he said while standing stiffly upright.

"Yes, sir," I said as I measured his height, neck, and waist. "What's your waist size?" I asked him.

"Not sure," he replied.

"Forty-two," I stated. "You are 3 percent over the body fat standards, sir." Requirements for men are 22 percent. For women, it is 30 percent.

His face reddened, and he stiffened up even more. "Well, uh," he stammered. "What are you going to do?"

"Sir," I replied, "this is your program. I'm a newcomer here. You are the commanding officer. But what I normally do, sir, is I give everyone ninety days to get down to body fat standards. If they are not within the Navy's body fat standards after ninety days, I normally document that in a letter and place them on the command physical readiness program."

He looked at me, still standing stiffly.

"Well, do your job, Petty Officer Cooley!"

"Sir, as of Monday you need to report to the PRT program," I said.

He turned and marched out. I couldn't believe it. I had just put the commanding officer of the base on the PRT program.

He did report to the program that following Monday. He followed the regimen and probably lost twenty-five pounds and 5 percent body fat over the next ninety days. A year later, he called me up during an awards ceremony.

"Petty Officer Cooley is a man of honor, integrity, and ethics," he said before giving me a Navy Commendation Medal. "I know that firsthand because when I checked into the command, I was over the body fat standard. He put me on the PRT program. Now if he's going to hold me, the commanding officer, to this standard, he had some guts and he would surely hold everyone else accountable."

I left Guam and headed to Recruit Training Command in Great Lakes, Illinois. Along with being a drill instructor and teaching new company commanders how to be drill instructors, I also stayed true to my passion of creating PRT programs so our sailors could obtain and maintain Navy standards. In addition, I had become a bodybuilder and a powerlifter. I was the number one powerlifter in my 181-pound weight class in the Midwest.

After winning another contest, our Navy base news team interviewed me. They asked if I would be interested in starting a five- to ten-minute daily segment for the news program called *Cooley's Fitness Tips*. This had a successful two-and-a-half-year run where I wrote, directed, and produced forty-seven episodes of the segment, which were viewed by more than one million sailors on the American Forces Network (AFN).

My fitness programs gained even greater notice, much to the dismay of some sailors, when I was on the USS *Blue Ridge*. There I developed another PRT program to keep the Seventh Fleet staff and shift company on the *Blue Ridge* in shape and working together. I was working out in the *Blue Ridge* gym one day when Vice Admiral Archie Clemins came up to me and started talking. I mentioned my idea that each member of the Seventh Fleet staff and *Blue Ridge* crew should physically train (PT) at least three days a week, regardless if they were at sea or on shore.

The admiral agreed and said he would be joining the PT sessions. Anytime the admiral does something like that, all others will follow. This became a requirement on board the *Blue Ridge*, and we became the first ship in the Navy where all members were required to work out three days a week.

The AFN came to Yokosuka, Japan, and did a story on me and the *Blue Ridge* fitness regimen. This caught the attention of the Navy's top officer, Admiral Michael Boorda, who came on board for a visit shortly afterward.

This was big news. The chief of naval operations never ever comes aboard your ship. It became even bigger news for me when the commanding officer of the ship and the chief of staff for the admiral of the Seventh Fleet came into my space, the Radio Shack.

My whole crew—everybody—froze.

"At ease! Where is Chief Cooley?" Captain Joy asked.

I started sweating, thinking, *What have I done?* The ship's captain and the chief of staff hardly ever came to the Radio Shack, and certainly not at the same time.

The admiral's chief of staff smiled a bit. "Chief Cooley, get your stuff together. Admiral Boorda wants to see you on the flight deck," he informed me.

We went up to the flight deck, and Admiral Boorda was there along with everyone else on the ship to make some announcements, including one to the entire Navy. He informed every sailor and officer that the *Blue Ridge* PRT program was being implemented Navy-wide and they would be required to participate in PRT at least three times a week. Up until this point, there had been no physical fitness requirement for the Navy as a whole. But truthfully, the Navy was the fattest, and he must have known it.

The AFN TV spot about the *Blue Ridge* PRT program and this announcement was shown around the world, and I became known as that guy who created this new requirement—"That guy who's making me PT three days a week!" My good intentions to try to make our Navy better by having the fittest sailors led me to become one of the more recognizable faces in the Navy, for both good and bad.

FROM THE OUTHOUSE TO THE WHITE HOUSE

Fifteen years after I started as a young enlisted sailor, I became an officer. I came up through the ranks the hard way, as AFN noted when they did a news story on the change of charge at the US Naval Air Facility in Misawa, Japan. I was leaving there after serving three years as the officer in charge to mold sailors in Hawaii. I had taken every opportunity to show my leadership ability and learn technical skills, combined with the Limited Duty Officer Program designed for senior petty or chief petty officers who have strong, specific technical knowledge and leadership experience, I was able to become a commissioned officer.

I was going to see life on both sides of the military fence. To prepare for the other side, I went to Officer Instructor Training, known as "knife and fork school." That's where the senior officers try to teach new officers' etiquette and how to conduct themselves. But I didn't mind. This had been a dream of mine since I joined the Navy.

Those of us coming up from the enlisted ranks were called "mustangs," and we were now with Navy guys who had graduated from the Naval Academy or from other programs that put them in the pipeline to become officers.

It was like going from peasant to aristocrat, and in my case, that was truer than with most other officers. I literally had been using an outhouse just thirty years before I would be working in the Pentagon and White House.

Me at the Navy officer candidate school, what we called "knife and fork school" (January 1995)

Now I said they tried to teach us etiquette in the wardroom where the officers dine. But it just didn't work. Sure enough, one of the mustangs would grab a chicken leg from another's plate. Or saw into a steak and make a mess of it.

Many times the captain would jokingly said, "Oh, that's disgusting. I can't teach you mustangs nothing!"

But we'd say, "Captain, you can't change us. We're mustangs. We came up from enlisted ranks."

The captain would smile, telling the young officers, "Do not follow their lead."

But the captain knew we were going to train the young academy officers to be great leaders in our Navy.

In Misawa, I had been designated the "officer in charge" of fifty-seven sailors. My command was responsible for providing various communication services to the Navy Patron Wing and Misawa's Navy. This was an extraordinary tour of duty. I saw my detachment win every communication readiness award three years in a row and experience a growth in promotions; and 99 percent of my sailors maintained PRT standards during my tour in Misawa.

Me with Admiral Archie Clemins on the date I was commissioned a United States Navy officer, January 1, 1995

When I was leaving my command there, my second class petty officer named Nelson Oconer, who worked for me for two years, was interviewed on the AFN news segment. "Mr. Cooley made me a better sailor," this young man said about my command. "I don't need anyone to tell me what to do. I just take initiative and get things done. And things that I know need to be done, I just take care of because Mr. Cooley showed me how to do that." (Oconer went on to make master chief petty officer within seventeen years and retired at the top of the enlisted ranks.)

To me, Petty Officer Oconer's comments meant that I'd taught my sailor well. At the end of their segment, AFN included a message

I gave to my sailors.

"My parting wish for you men and women of my detachment is that you will place your faith [in our Lord], develop your personal version of the world, and see life not as it is but how it should be."

My United States Navy picture as I was promoted to lieutenant (o3e)

My next station assignment would be Oahu, Hawaii, where the Naval Computer and Telecommunications Area Master Station Pacific (NCTAMS PAC) is headquartered.

I was assigned to be the assistant officer in charge (AOIC) at Camp H.M. Smith outside of the headquarters at Wahiawa and went to work for Bernadette Semple. Semple was a good friend I met in Guam when she was a lieutenant junior grade and I was a first class petty officer.

We were responsible for all communications in support of the chief in charge of the Pacific Fleet, twenty-three general officers (generals and admirals), seven detachments, and over 600 sailors and civilians.

This was an awesome assignment until our commanding officer, who was headquartered in Wahiawa, decided she wanted to run one of the largest communication commands, in support of the commander of the Seventh Fleet and the Western Pacific, with all-white female officers in charge of all major activities in this part of the world.

Therefore, the captain started reassigning her black officers to the Planning Department at headquarters. This department was considered the kiss of death for a career and would negatively affect an officer's record when it came time for evaluations and promotions.

During this time in our Navy, in 1998 and 1999, the Navy 1700 community, primarily non-surface (non-shipboard) personnel and mostly 90 percent female, consisted of mostly white women, many of who were having a hard time adjusting to leadership positions at sea and some major commands.

The Navy was thinking about reducing the 1700 job community or possibly eliminating it all together. I believe my captain wanted to show the Navy that she could run a major command with all white women in key positions in order to save this community.

Most of the black officers, both men and women, were assigned to the Planning Department except me. Since I was about twenty-five miles away from Wahiawa at Camp Smith, the captain had forgotten that she had not reassigned me until she visited one day and noticed that I was still filling the position as AOIC there.

"Lieutenant Cooley, why aren't you reassigned to Fleet Technical Operation Center?" she asked. Before I could say, she continued, "well, I want you to report there immediately. I will assign another lieutenant to replace you in your current assignment."

This is when all hell broke loose. A claim followed, as did national attention, to racial discrimination in the Navy. The drama and outcome could fill another chapter, if not another book, and is something I plan to share in a future publication.

The most important takeaway from this time of my Navy career is how it enforced the power of conviction. If you really, truly believe that something isn't right, you must stick with that belief and be prepared to shout your truth from every rooftop, in front of those at the highest levels of our government, until someone finally hears you.

The end of my Navy career took me to Washington, DC, where I served in both the Pentagon and stood duty at the White House.

I was around the top decision makers in the country and the world. I had the opportunity to encounter then-President Bill Clinton and First Lady Hillary Clinton. I listened to Colin Powell, the former US Secretary of State and four-star Army general, speak at several events and even sat down and talked with him.

I found him to be a very approachable man and a genuine person through and through.

The way I do my speeches today was influenced by watching Mr. Powell. I've never seen him get up on stage with notes, but he does not miss a beat. He would speak for an hour and a half without a single note, and no teleprompters either.

I used to have my speeches written out and rehearsed. Then I got to thinking about Mr. Powell and how he did it.

You have to understand the flow of what you're saying and trying to convey, and you have to be able to improvise based on your audience. It's just like being a stand-up comedian, which I was for years throughout my Navy career. (It's true. My gift for gab and my reputation as a jokester followed me around from base to base. I would open for notable comedians like Sinbad, Simply Marvelous, Mark Curry, Cedric the Entertainer, Anthony Roysters, and all of the Bay Area comedians. Eventually, I became soured by the drugs and selfishness I saw in the Hollywood world and decided I did not want to be in the spotlight that way.)

Watching Mr. Powell, you knew what he was saying was coming from the heart and was true to him. Politics aside, whether you agreed with him or not, he truly meant what he was saying, deep down in his core. And if that's the case, then you don't need notes. You just speak from your heart.

That's what my speaking engagements are based on now. Everything that I talk about comes from the heart. If I don't feel it, I cannot share it. If it's not true to me, I am not going to tell anyone about it.

We must speak, educate, and, most importantly, influence our next generation based on our experiences and our belief that we can make this world a better place by showing respect, caring, and consideration for all.

TIMELINE OF MY NAVY CAREER

Twenty-three years | one month | twenty-two days as a sailor and officer in the United States Navy

- **September 10, 1978** Boarded a bus from Chattanooga to boot camp in Orlando, Florida
- **March 1979** USS Barney, based in Norfolk, Virginia
- **May 1980** Navy Communication Area Master Station
- **Shore duty due to thyroid cancer** *1980-1982*
- **Exmouth, Australia** *1982-1984*
    - Basketball and rugby player for the Navy Base Team
    - Second Class Radioman
    - Technical Controller
- **Moffett Field, Bay Area, California** *1984-1987*
    - PRT Coordinator
    - Stand-up comedian
    - Second Class Radioman
- **Guam** *1987-1989*
    - First Class Radioman
    - Leader of Rifle Funeral Detail
    - Command Fitness Coordinator

- **Great Lakes, Illinois** (the Navy's only boot camp) *1989-1993*
    - Writer, director, and producer of Cooley's Fitness Tips, broadcast to more than one million viewers in the Navy
    - Established a first-of-its-kind breakfast tutoring program for underprivileged at-risk youths at a local elementary school
    - Received the Point of Light award for community service established by President George H.W. Bush

Being awarded the Admiral Gallery and Admiral Rankin awards, which included the first Presidential Point of Light nomination in 1992

- *Blue Ridge* (the command ship of the United States Seventh Fleet) based in Yokosuka, Japan *1993-1995*
    - Established first Navy-wide at-sea physical fitness program
    - Closed out enlisted record as master chief petty officer (E-9)

- **Commissioned Naval Officer** *1995-2001*
    - Officer in Charge, US Naval Air Facility, Misawa, Japan
    - Assistant Officer in Charge—Camp Smith
    - Oahu, Hawaii—Division Officer
    - Washington, DC—Operations Officer N-6 Pentagon, worked with White House communications;
    - Director of Education and Training at Commander, Naval Telecommunication Agency
    - Retired with rank of Lieutenant (O3E)

PART IV:
A NEW PATH

"Because I believe Mr. Cooley's program is so successful at motivating the youth and giving them the tools they need to be successful in their academic and their adult careers, I would recommend Mr. Cooley . . . to not take no for an answer."

—good advice from my former intern, Erica Pereida

SOARING TO NEW HEIGHTS

When I was forty-one, several events came together at once in my life. I was single again after my second marriage ended and my two youngest children, my eight-year-old daughter and three-year-old son, came to live with me. I had a hip replacement. And despite the fact I was working in the Pentagon as director of Naval Education and Training, I decided it was time to leave the Navy. I was immediately offered a job at Computer Science Center Incorporated (CSCI), a government contractor assigned to the Pentagon, making more money than I ever dreamed was possible.

I worked on great assignments that helped develop and create our next-generation missile controls, replacement ships for our future Navy, and many other engineering programs that I cannot talk about because of security and confidentiality reasons. I worked for CSCI for almost two years before Lockheed Martin approached me to take a job as one of the original design engineers for the Joint Strike Fighter Program, the F-35 program.

The following two aircraft are beyond impressive in their capabilities—and in their price tags. The Lockheed Martin F-22 Raptor is a stealth tactical fighter aircraft we developed for the

United States Air Force at a price of $150 million per plane. The F-35 plane is a stealth multirole fighter designed for ground attack and air superiority missions. It emerged from the Joint Strike Fighter Program that intended to replace a variety of aircraft for the US military and our allies. With a program cost of more than $1.5 trillion, it is considered the largest and most expensive military program in US history.

Both are extremely powerful planes, designed to fly undetected. By the time an enemy does see them, it's too late for them to do anything.

Drawing on the crypto and technology knowledge I gained in the Navy, I became a lead crypto graphics engineer on these projects. My work encompassed the design of key e-crypto equipment and algorithms that control the missiles and other weapons and communications of the airplane.

This work requires top-secret special-access clearance. If you don't have it, you're not part of the program. Only about ten of us had that level of understanding, and I was the only African-American lead crypto engineer in Lockheed Martin at that time.

And this was a big position otherwise. I controlled the certification of design for these programs, meaning if your design was not certified and accredited, then you had an expensive weapon that could not be used.

Standing with my design team with our design of the prototype for the F-35 (Joint Strike Fighter) plane for Lockheed Martin

We had to lay out milestones to the government and continuously justify to Congress why we should keep this program alive.

Many roadblocks and setbacks occurred on the F-35 project, as you can easily find out with an internet search. It's almost inevitable, with a project of that scope and cost. Even with seemingly insurmountable challenges, I rallied my team to stay focused on our end goal. We made it through Milestone B, or halfway completed, before I left Lockheed Martin to take an executive position working on a next-generation crypto operability super radio system. I worked for two years doing that until the Lord had a new path for me that became clear: the vision for The JC Cooley Foundation.

REPAIRING OLD WOUNDS

Beyond the poverty and racism that countless other African-Americans have endured, I also persevered through forty-eight surgeries so I could eventually breathe and speak normally again.

This was a nine-year ordeal that started out as a simple case of sleep apnea where your breathing stops and starts while you're sleeping. I had to use a CPAP machine and wear a full facial mask to help me breathe, but I just could not deal with it. I would wake up in the middle of the night, startled and trying to pull that clunky thing off my face. I would eventually stop using it.

I transferred to another location of Lockheed Martin in the Dallas, Texas, area and met with a doctor there who wanted to remove my adenoids, some of my soft palate, and part of my tonsils, as well as repair a deviated septum.

There was a fifty-fifty chance these procedures would work and I would be free from the CPAP machine, so I had the surgery. Seven days later, the packing used in my nostrils after surgery was removed. "You should be able to breathe now," the doctor said.

But I couldn't.

I took extra steroids to reduce any swelling that might remain, and I waited for another week or so to see if that helped.

It didn't.

I could only breathe through my mouth, and I could not talk normally. I was told I had a problem seen only in babies. There were no other cases like mine, and there was nothing for the doctors I consulted with to compare it to. They could give me a trachea (a hole in the neck), or they could try and rebuild my nasal system from scratch. But they didn't know what those odds were.

Another doctor tried a skin graft, thinking perhaps cells from my own body would help in the healing process. They literally took a piece of skin from my behind—you can imagine the joke that resulted, me having a piece of my own butt in my mouth—but it didn't take.

Therefore, I developed keloids, or thick scar tissue where my body tried to heal itself. Every two weeks the hole at the top of my mouth would close automatically, also called stenosis. When this would happen, doctors would perform surgery and open it back up. This meant that half of what I was eating or drinking would make its way into my stomach and the other half would come out my nose. I used to have to eat over a bucket. I remember one night my son Joshua, who was seven years old at that time, came into my bedroom where I was eating dinner. He thought I was a magician. He also realized then that Daddy had a real problem, and he ran out of the room.

Eventually, my doctor decided my only option was to have an oral and maxillofacial surgeon who specializes in treating the head, neck, face, and jaws, in addition to an ear, nose, and throat (ENT) specialist together in the same operating room. But first, I would have to find an oral and maxillofacial surgeon. Then I would have to find a way to pay for it or get it approved somehow through my military insurance benefits, which would only pay for the ENT.

At this time, I recall there were only 182 of these oral and maxillofacial specialists in the United States, and three of them happened to be in San Diego at the Naval Regional Medical Center. I almost couldn't believe my luck.

When I called, the receptionist informed me there were no appointments for a year.

This little ray of light dimmed. My life was over, I thought, imagining another year of eating over a bucket and washing out my sinuses and throat afterward to prevent infection. Another year of not being able to sleep for more than an hour or two because I could only breathe through my mouth.

I decided that my new wife, Michelle, and I would fly to San Diego and go to the Naval Medical Center, also known as Balboa Naval Hospital, and make them tell me no in person. I arrived in San Diego on a Monday and was in the surgeon's office by eight thirty a.m.

I sat outside Dr. Carpenter's office, hoping to catch his eye and talk with him.

He came out at one point and asked me who I was there to see.

"Well, you," I answered.

"You? You're not on my schedule," he said as he looked at his chart.

"No, I'm not," I replied.

"I can't see you. My schedule is full for the next year."

I positioned myself in a place where he had to walk by me anytime he went into the office lobby.

When the clock hit three p.m., I was still sitting in the same seat. A little while later, the doctor finished up with his last patient.

"What do you want?" he said. "Why are you still here?"

"The Lord told me to come and see you," I said. "I came all the way from Dallas to see you."

"I don't care who told you to come and see me," he replied. "I don't have any appointments! Why didn't you call and save yourself some time?"

"I did."

"Alright," he said, looking toward the folder I had in my hand. "Let me see what you've got."

I gave him a folder several inches thick. As he flipped through it, his eyes got bigger and bigger.

"Forty-two surgeries!"

At that moment, I believe he saw a potential opportunity because Balboa Naval Hospital is a training facility for resident doctors to perfect their skills in their chosen medical career paths.

He picked up the phone and called the Balboa Hospital head ENT specialist, Captain Jones.

Just like I thought, they saw this as a training opportunity for the residents. Apparently, I would be a good one because they had never seen a case like the one I presented.

I signed some papers that allowed me to be their test case and get me started on a new battery of surgeries. They told me I was going to need six or seven more surgeries, and it still might not work.

My job was now in the Dallas/Fort Worth area, and I was looking at a lot of back and forth to the hospital in San Diego when two months later, Lockheed Martin received a new contract and needed someone to head up a multibillion-dollar assurance project in that area. My bosses said they thought I'd be perfect for it.

An opportunity like that, in the very same area where I needed to get my surgeries done—I could hardly believe it.

God is good, I thought.

So they moved me and Michelle to La Jolla, California, just miles from where I would get my treatments.

On September 10, 2009, doctors finished the battery of surgeries and finally got it right! Ironically, September 10 is the day I went into the Navy thirty-one years earlier. I had to go in for six more surgeries to perform tweaks, but there were no more major surgeries or hospital stays. At this point, my sinus passages had literally been rebuilt.

During all of this, I had people positioned around the world working on my teams for Lockheed Martin. After one of my surgeries, a large and very important meeting had been scheduled. As soon as I came out of surgery and woke up, I asked Michelle to patch me in to a conference call.

I was in the recovery room and tried to lead this meeting. But I couldn't talk, much less make any sense with all the medication that remained in my system just two hours after surgery. A few coworkers I was close to figured out what was going on, and they tried to help me out during the meeting. Later, they told me that everyone on the call had been puzzled, trying to figure out what I was saying.

I have always been dedicated to anything I am doing. I believed that this was my team and that this program was so important that I needed to be the only one leading this effort, regardless of my health.

Michelle had tried to take the phone away and stop me from calling in, but I was too caught up in my job. I was determined, despite what it might cost me in my relationship, health, or recovery. When I am committed to something I'm committed, but I realized this was to an extreme.

I learned something very important that day: Everyone in an organization is replaceable, and the corporate system really does not care about you, only your production and the value you bring at that moment.

The entire experience—from the initial surgeries and not knowing if I would ever eat, breathe, sleep, or talk normally again, to leading a meeting just hours after I woke up—made me realize how precious and fleeting life can be. And how misplaced my priorities had been.

This is not a book about romance or love. There are thousands upon thousands of novels and essays and memoirs about that emotion and the crazy and wonderful things it can cause men and women to do. Just like with my Navy career, I could fill an entire book with my experiences and what I learned from my three marriages.

But I must share a bit so you can meet one of the most beautiful, kindhearted women I've been blessed to know.

My first wife, Sharon, had been my high school sweetheart. A year behind me in school, she was still a senior when I enlisted in the Navy. No surprise, I was young and naive. At the age of nineteen, alone and away from home for the first time, I asked her to marry me and come to live with me in Norfolk, Virginia.

She quickly got lonely herself and decided to return to Chattanooga to her family after the birth of our first son, James III. After almost three years of her living in Chattanooga while I lived in Norfolk, she returned to Virginia. This was right before I enlisted for four more years and the Navy transferred me to my first overseas assignment in Australia. We were living in naval base housing for about eighteen months when my wife became pregnant again. With less than six months left on this tour in Australia, she asked me to send her back to Chattanooga to live with her parents. This hurt me so deeply but I wanted her to be happy, so I sent her home.

I transferred to Moffett Field in the Bay Area one month before the due date of our second son, D'Angelo. I rented a very nice place about two miles from the base. I asked her to come to the Bay Area to have the baby, which she did. Soon after the baby was born though, she wanted to move back to Chattanooga to be around her family, not recognizing that I and our two sons *were* her family.

Right then I knew that I could not live like this—not knowing if my wife would ever want to make our family her number one priority.

I let her move back to Chattanooga, and six months later I went home for a visit. When I arrived at her apartment, another man answered the door in his underwear.

I told her she could have whatever she wanted, and I went down to the courthouse and filed for divorce. For some reason, she asked to keep the several VCRs we owned and I gladly gave them to her.

Seven years, two months, and two days of marriage were over.

Years later, I would get married again to a young lady I met when I was stationed in Guam. We would have two children together, Brittany and Joshua, and were married for almost nine years when things went south. Military life is hard enough, much less with a spouse who is also in the service. Maybe it just wasn't meant to be—for me to have a spouse and the life of a Navy officer at the same time.

We divorced, and two years later she dropped off my two youngest children to live with me in DC.

I was devastated. I had to examine myself from a personal perspective to try and figure out what I was doing wrong because I consider myself 100 percent dedicated and committed to everything I do or try to do. After that, I swore I was never going to get married again. That was it. I was done.

Then one day in May 2006, I was in a Macy's department store in Atlanta with my best friend, Billy Harper. I had been going back and forth from Atlanta for work and to spend time with him, and this day we decided to go to Lenox Mall. It was my lucky day. As we were shopping, I noticed a beautiful young lady.

And there I met her: Michelle Freeman. Originally from New York, she was living in Atlanta, where some of her family members had settled.

Michelle was intelligent, calm, thoughtful, and had caring eyes that instantly drew me in.

Naturally, I was going to get close enough to have a chat with her. I went up to her, smiling and pretending to be a perfume salesman. I asked her if she wanted to try some samples.

She looked at me, smiling back, and said, "You are not a salesman in this store because I come here all the time."

I grinned, admitting that, no, I was not a perfume salesman.

We talked for about five minutes before I asked her for her phone number. She declined but said I could give her my phone number. I gave her every number I had—my cell, my home, and my work numbers.

I watched her as she walked away. Billy and I then went to a few more stores and as luck would have it ran into Michelle again, who was with her good friend Traci.

"Are you following me around?" I asked her.

Michelle laughed.

"Okay, well, don't forget to give me a call," I said.

She looked at me, smiled, and walked away.

I flew back home to Dallas the next day. One week later, she emailed me and later on called me. And we have talked every single day since.

We started dating, and she would travel back and forth between Atlanta and Texas to see me. After two years of that, we decided to get married. It took some perseverance, as all good things in life do, and it almost didn't happen. The week of our wedding, our family and friends gathered in Atlanta for our ceremony, to be held on March 15. The day before the big day, we went out to get a marriage license, thinking we had all the necessary paperwork and documents. But no clerk or judge would grant us one because they said they needed an original copy of my divorce decree from Hawaii. We drove all around the state practically, pleading our case until we found a judge who would finally listen to us. She said, "If you guys get married right now, this very minute, I'll sign it." So we exchanged marriage vows almost immediately.

Me and my beautiful wife Michelle Cooley on our wedding day, March 15, 2008

The following day, we got married again in the church, giving us two wedding dates.

Billy remembers that I was definitely not looking for anyone when Michelle just happened to show up that day at the Macy's store in Lenox Mall and be the right person for me. She supports me 100 percent, he says, which I know is no easy task.

I'll admit it hasn't always been a smooth ride, especially at first. It's fair to say I was a bit gun-shy given my previous relationships. And it's also hard to join together as a couple. But after several years, we became locked into place as one unit. We began working together with one vision, one focus, and one goal. If you have that unity, you can accomplish anything together.

Another important factor in our relationship is that I have finally learned the eighty-twenty rule: If you find someone you like 80 percent of the time, grab them tight and don't let them go because you will never *ever* be satisfied 100 percent of the time. We all have strengths and weaknesses that we do and don't like about the other person.

Luckily, I have more than 80 percent happiness in my relationship today. Michelle is truly a marvelous woman who God sent into my life to help mold me, guide me, and calm me down—and most importantly to teach me the meaning of love.

When I first met Michelle, I was extremely driven. Kind of like the drill instructor I had once been, I was constantly striving for perfection, to reach that next level, almost at any cost. I expected everyone to be committed and determined to succeed just like I was, but the world is not like that.

I have softened in the fourteen years since I have met her and have learned to follow my heart. She has helped me adjust my attitude and discover what a kind heart looks like. She has made me softer and better all around, and I thank God every single day for giving me this shining star. I also must thank Billy for taking me to the mall that day so I could meet her.

DARING TO DREAM BIG, THINK BIG, AND BE BIG

During this time, I started to dream big, think big, and most importantly *be* big. I began investing in real estate, thanks to some encouragement from and friendly competition with Billy, and pursued other business ventures. I also began practicing public speaking at Toastmasters and at any community and service organization that would allow me to speak in more formal settings. That gift of gab was still there from my comedian days, and it seemed like if I had five minutes, I could have the crowd.

I also started thinking about the kids out there who are in a similar situation to the one I had been in as a young boy. They might have no guidance and no direction and think there is no way out of the environment in which they are living. But I knew different because I am an example of what it takes to rise above your environment, no matter the situation.

Michelle and I settled in Temecula, California, a city in south Riverside County about an hour north of San Diego. I started reaching out to Rotary Clubs, Boys & Girls Clubs, churches, and schools to try to speak to youths and young adults, and adults as well, to help them to see another path.

Speaking at the Bethlehem Community Center in Chattanooga, returning after 45 years to tell the youth of today they can do anything they set their minds to

This hadn't been my original plan, but when I started to observe the takeaways for the kids and their parents, my heart just changed. I had an epiphany: *This is what I'm supposed to be doing*, I felt—sharing my experiences, my successes, and my failures with others in case they are going through something similar.

I started fine-tuning my different philosophies. What I was trying to express, what had built up inside of me for the last fifty-four years, started making sense, and it seemed to click with the groups I spoke with.

But it was slow going at first. I tried for several years to build up an audience and speaking engagements.

Then onto this path came Don Dickinson, a retired business owner and real estate mogul, who I met at the Temecula 24 Hour Fitness center. I would go to this gym almost daily and created quite a following as I used the steam room, sauna, and relaxed in the Jacuzzi. Many members seemed to know my schedule and when I would be around these areas during my three-to-four-hour stay at the gym. Of all the things I have been called in my life, I can also say I am known as the "Mayor of 24 Hour Fitness."

One day, Don, who I had not met before, had been watching as I spoke with some of the folks who had come to talk to me. He asked me if I was a preacher. I replied that I was not.

Don then asked me if I would be interested in speaking at his Rotary Club. I said that I would.

And with that one invitation, a whole new path would emerge for me.

Don's Rotary Club was fifteen miles south of Temecula in Fallbrook, a small town tucked away in the rocky hills of northern San Diego County where avocados grow in abundance and the old ways of country and farming life still remain.

My speech was to be given at the exclusive Grand Tradition Estate and Gardens, and when Don invited me, I quickly found out I would be the first black speaker to grace its grounds.

Michelle and I arrived at the Grand Tradition Rotary Club around eleven forty-five a.m. It was amusing to hear the members say, "You must be James Cooley, our speaker for today."

I had been invited to speak at this Rotary Club without any of its board members requesting my resume, but I had brought copies of it along with a copy of my prepared speech.

The club president then announced that my resume had been placed on each table and that everyone should read it.

As the members did so, I heard mumblings in the audience of mostly older, wealthy white men.

I swear I heard comments like, "I've never seen a black man so educated!"

"A lieutenant?!"

Each time after a member would speak or a presentation finished during the program, the club president would remind the members to please take the time to read my resume before I spoke. I became annoyed after the fourth time he said this.

In front of 200 to 300 folks, as the first black speaker at this venue, I would soon talk about my background. But first I had to get something off my chest.

I looked at Michelle, folded my prepared speech, and decided to let the crowd know how I felt about their reaction to and their judgment of me—emotions they felt without even knowing how I had become the educated and successful person my resume reflected.

"Okay, you've now seen my bio. Now let me tell you what's *not* on the bio. Imagine a scenario where you're in the library, looking for a book on love. You ask the librarian, and she says, 'We've got a million books on love, but we have a pile on the table. Everything you want to know about love is there,' she tells you. So you grab a hardback from some raggedy-looking books and you see a couple more raggedy books and throw them away.

"That's how I felt about you guys reading my bio," I told the crowd. "You guys don't know anything about me other than what you read on that paper. Try to look at what's on the inside before you judge me. You guys judged me, and you didn't know me. I was one of the raggedy books you tried to throw to the side. Never judge a book by its cover, and that's what you guys did to me.

"I think its racist, I'm just going to say it," I continued. "I apologize for the harsh words, but that's how I feel. Now let me tell you what's not in the book . . ."

They rose and gave me a standing ovation. I told them about my upbringing in Alabama and Chattanooga, about my career in the Navy, and my perspectives on life—and certainly about not judging a book by its cover.

After my speech, Don told me that he wanted to help others discover who James Cooley is. He advised me to create a nonprofit organization to offer programs to build up youths, not just in Temecula but hopefully throughout the entire country one day.

He reached out to other organizations to help get me speaking engagements and introduced me to his best friend, Ron Walton, who would become one of my biggest supporters. He also introduced me to many of our city leaders who would eventually help me create what is now my foundation.

On Thanksgiving Day 2013, Michelle and I invited twenty people over to our house for dinner, including Don and two homeless people from under a nearby bridge.

Halfway through our meal, Don stood up and asked everyone for their undivided attention. He asked me to come over. Not expecting anything from him, he reached into his shirt pocket and pulled out a check for $25,000 and announced, "JC Cooley, it is now time for you to go out there and set the stage for your foundation!"

I was stunned and reluctant to accept the money, but he assured me that nothing was expected in return.

"Just go and do your thing and help others who may not know which direction they are headed. That is all," he said.

This is when the foundation's name came to me: The JC Cooley Foundation–Options & Opportunities: The Choice Program. It was a vision that Don and I discussed many times since we first met at the Jacuzzi in the 24 Hour Fitness in Temecula.

On February 1, 2015, we held our first program with sixty-five youths and their parents, and Don gave opening remarks. "Approximately eleven months ago, I walked into the Jacuzzi at the gym and I met Mr. James Cooley and it changed my life." He stopped there for just a moment, with a catch in his throat, before continuing, "And he will change your life too, if you will let him.

The JC Cooley Foundation monthly breakfast program encourages youths to Dream Big, Think Big and Be Big. I hope these fine young people left with that message (March 2018)

Approximately six months ago, James decided that he was going to give the rest of his life to serve the youth of this nation. You have the privilege of being the first at our youth program."

As the foundation has grown and developed, we have hosted frequent breakfasts for local youths to motivate and inspire them. We have given scholarships to help graduating seniors on their path to achieving a higher education. In our first year, we gave three scholarships. In our next year, we gave fifteen. We have now given over 200 scholarships to date.

I speak at schools throughout Southern California, at local business groups, Rotary Clubs, and wherever else we can bring value, averaging forty to fifty speaking engagements a year.

Speaking to over 400 fifth graders at a Temecula, California elementary school about what it takes to be a leader in America (May 2019)

The foundation has also partnered with universities such as California State University San Marcos and the University of Southern California, where I work with professors to place students in internships with the foundation and give them experience working with youths and a nonprofit organization.

One of my previous interns, Erica Pereida, was finishing her degree at Cal State San Marcos and making plans to pursue a career in social work. Erica had come from the foster system and wanted to help foster youths in schools. She attended nearly every breakfast and program we hosted. She took photos, wrote synopses of the events, and helped in any other way she could. She also mentored and tutored several foster students in afterschool programs I had arranged in area high schools.

For one of her last classes at Cal State San Marcos, she wrote a paper on the experience and made a video of herself addressing several questions about what the foundation did well and what it could do better.

She talked about her pride in working with struggling students who ended up earning enough credits to pass their classes and graduate.

Through my messages and speeches, she noted how the foundation and I, give the youths "that extra push to do what they already can do. He's just helping them realize their potential."

I can't think of any better compliment.

She had some recommendations for me too. "Because I believe Mr. Cooley's program is so successful at motivating the youth and giving them the tools they need to be successful in their academic and their adult careers, I would recommend Mr. Cooley . . . to not take no for an answer. His program is beneficial for all youth at all ages.

"A lot of times people don't want to hear him out about what the program stands for," she continued. "So that's part of saying he should not take 'no' for an answer, and he should keep being persistent because his program does deserve to be spread across . . . everywhere."

I think I will take her advice.

PART V:
MY PHILOSOPHIES

Dream Big, Think Big, Be Big

—motto of The JC Cooley Foundation

INTRODUCTION TO MY PHILOSOPHIES: THE 6 T'S

As I mentioned previously, as I got older I realized that I needed to follow my heart, which had changed course as I shifted from life in the Navy to careers as a corporate executive, government contractor, and small business owner.

As I followed certain paths, I always knew that it was not me leading the way down them. I was following the beliefs that I had learned from an early age, going back to that six-year-old boy in Alabama who would listen to the tales, wisdom, and admonishments of, especially, his Grandma Mattie, Uncle Robert, and Aunt Gen.

The rule in Graham was that we would go to church—and I mean go almost every day. I always knew God had a purpose for me. But I would not listen to him the way a true believer should. Therefore, I had many lessons to learn, as you have already read and will learn more about in the following pages.

The many paths I have walked down, with all their twists and turns and triumphs and tribulations, have led me to come up with certain philosophies and beliefs that I think apply to all of us.

I bring these messages to the teens and young adults at the weekend programs and other events hosted by The JC Cooley Foundation–Options & Opportunities: The Choice Program and at school presentations and programs we are asked to participate in. I share them with youths' parents and with community members at Rotary Clubs and other organizations where I am invited to speak.

I hope they have found these messages inspiring and have come away with at least a little guidance and motivation. I hope you will too.

Today, I am a believer from the bottom of my heart and with every ounce of energy I have in my body. I believe God led me down these paths to teach me about successes and failures. Therefore, my philosophies that you will read about in the following pages are based on my premise of the 6 T's:

1) Trumpets
2) Trials
3) Turbulence
4) Tested
5) Triumph, and most importantly
6) Testaments

The first T begins with a warning sign. Many times in our lives, we get a feeling that something just isn't right and we get signs from God that try to alert us that problems could be coming unless we take some action—you know, like that little nag, that knot in your stomach about not paying bills or going to the doctor.

These are *trumpets*, and many times we ignore their call of caution. Therefore, failing in this T causes great pain in our lives.

The second T, *trials*, starts when we fail to listen to warning signs. This will lead to us experiencing some other T's that I call sub T's:

- Tribulations, where many other trials are added on
- Temptation, the dark side where I believe the devil can lead you into making a bad decision
- Temporary fix, where problems are not fixed and trials return

Turbulence is the third T. This happens when we have doubt and are not willing to give 100 percent. Imagine that passage from the Bible where Jesus and his disciples are on a boat becoming engulfed by the waters from a violent storm. The disciples wake him up, fearing they are going to drown. "You of little faith, why are you so afraid?" he asks them. So he gets up and calms the waters and wind. We must continue having faith, even when the waters are getting rough. We have to withstand the turbulence and make it across to the other side.

Once we get safely to dry land, that brings us to the fourth T, *tested*. But being tested does not mean victory. Many of us fall back in the same situation that we were just in. We must continue to walk the path, pray, and stay on course. Many of us go through a challenging situation or circumstance and scream out for God. Now he is a God of faith and guides us to victory, but once we reach safety, many of us will go back to doing the same thing that caused the problem in the first place.

Triumph comes when we maintain the lessons learned from four of the six T's that we just talked about. We must stay true to ourselves, remember the lessons that God taught us, and once we have stayed on course, we may throw our hands up and say, "Victory!" We've reached the fifth T, *triumph*. But we're not done yet.

Being triumphant doesn't do anyone any good unless you are able to fulfill the sixth T, *testify*, and tell someone about it. Someone may be experiencing the same problems you have just been through, and by telling them your story, you might be able to save them from going through three or four of the 6 T's. We must share our stories as the people of the world share their stories about Jesus.

We must try and make this world a better place. We must do everything in our power to promote love and not hate and make ourselves better people, while helping others do the same. The 6 T's gives us a roadmap to accomplish all of those things.

FOCUS IS KEY

In the previous chapter, we talked about the six T's and how sometimes we lose focus on the things that are important and move us forward in life and how we lose our way with God or our maker.

In this chapter, I am going to talk about focus. I believe that focusing on the end result is of first and foremost importance to assist us in completing our tasks and achieving our goals.

Remember this: Focus is key. It's the key to completing anything you do and reaching your goals. It's the key to finding your destiny—I talk more about this extremely important task, and the important difference between destination and destiny, later in this section.

But focus will only work if you have two other necessary components: *vision* and *understanding*.

To begin any plan or project, you must define your goal and timeline. Action follows from there. I have learned that to move forward with reaching a goal, I must be able to see the end results in my mind's eye. If I want to build a house or a building, for example, I would have to understand the size, shape, and framework to move forward. I call this *vision*. You may not be able to actually see something because it's not in front of you, but you can come up with the framework of how you want it to look in your mind's eye. This takes us to *understanding*. Once you have a vision of what you are planning to build, understanding the resources needed will help you create a plan that includes time, money, and the schedule to complete the project.

But it's not going to come easy. You will have roadblocks. You will be thrown off course, and you will have to readjust, sometimes several times. That's where focus comes back in.

Often, we lose focus and are not able to complete our plan so we can move on to our next destination. Being able to focus comes from self-discipline. In my opinion, if you don't have that, you have little chance at succeeding because you will find at the end of the day that all you've been is scattered and you haven't really completed anything.

And sometimes we have to be able to push the weeds to the side and look for the jewel, for the opportunities, that might be waiting for us. That can be hard to do, but that's why focus is key—so you won't lose sight of that jewel.

I ran for a seat on the Temecula City Council in 2014 and for mayor in 2016. My main message in 2014 was "Focus is key." Michelle and I have developed a strong bond with this wonderful community and felt my leadership and life experiences could give it another, stronger voice. I had a good run in both elections but did not win a seat. Nonetheless, I continue to work to spread my message about focus, vision, and understanding to this city and to my audiences as far and wide as I can reach them.

OUR BIRTHRIGHTS

I believe we are all born in the image of our Lord Jesus Christ and that we all have the same common birthrights, regardless of race, color, creed, or religion. No matter the circumstances we may have been born into—poverty or wealth, country of origin, our parents, either good or bad—God created us equally and equipped every one of us with the tools that we need to be successful. The Birthrights are:

- Confidence
- Courage
- Hope
- Belief, and most importantly
- Faith

Confidence is the ability to be sure of who you are and know you have a purpose to fulfill on this earth just by being born and created in God's image.

Courage begins with the fact that none of us is born a coward. We are all born with the strengths that will allow us to pursue the many destinations we will encounter in pursuit of our ultimate destiny. We must be able to confide in our maker for the direction we need to start our journey of life.

Hope is the glue that keeps us together and focused on pursuing our purpose. As long as we maintain hope, we maintain the desire to move forward. Hope inspires us to dream and not give up on our goals or destiny. In my opinion, hope is one of the most important of these five birthrights.

Belief is something deep in our genes. I believe that God plants a unique gene in each of us and allows us to pursue our own purposes in our own ways. I believe no two people, not even twins, have the same exact beliefs and personality. This gene makes every one of us God's own masterpiece. Belief along with hope allows us to know that God has created a plan for us and that we have a unique purpose.

Faith means that for us to truly know that God created us in his image and has a plan for us, we must have faith in our maker. All the things we are born to do through these birthrights can be accomplished as long as we maintain faith in our maker. One thing I always wonder when I think about *not* having faith is that if there is no God, what gives you purpose for waking up and achieving your goals?

THE 4 C'S

I have *created* a saying that sums up what I believe are the building blocks of character and success.

I *collaborated* with others in forming these ideas and turning them into a song.

I *commit* to this saying, to these beliefs, with every part of me. When I say it, when I sing it, it comes from the deepest part of my heart. I believe others can feel that. I say it with *confidence*.

Create, collaborate, commit with confidence. That's what I call the 4 C's.

Here's what I mean by them:

Create: We have all these thoughts, all these ideas that have come to us, and sometimes we can be afraid to even talk about or entertain them because we think they are so far-fetched that someone is going to laugh at us. But don't care what people think. Explore your dreams and ideas with every ounce of creativity in you.

Collaborate: So you have these dreams and ideas and you might be the person to solve world hunger (I'm all about dreaming big, after all), but you don't want to share them. If you collaborate with others, you just might discover someone else who has the same dream as you and find a partner on your path.

Commit: If you have a vision, don't let anyone tell you that you can't do it. Be committed to it, and to yourself. Always believe in yourself and your goals.

Communicate with Confidence: This is a big part of staying focused and certainly the most important factor in collaboration. Tell others what you are doing. Get them on board your ship (yes, that's an old Navy term). The more you talk about it, the clearer and more defined your vision becomes. Have confidence in yourself and your vision.

I use the story of Mark Zuckerberg and the development of Facebook in my presentations as it illustrates several of my messages.

As he was developing Facebook from a dorm room in Harvard University, the concept came from existing creativity that resulted in the creation of an earlier social networking website, Myspace. He collaborated with his friends and peers, which made his idea and the algorithms stronger and better. He was committed to his vision even when he was told several times it wasn't going to work.

I feel this is such an important message that I collaborated with my good friend Charles Vienn, who put these 4 C's to music. You can hear it on my Facebook and YouTube pages.

ACE

Here's my definition of how to ACE life.

The **A** stands for Attitude. The **C** stands for Commitment. The **E** is for Enthusiasm.

> **A:** Attitude will make or break you. Let's think about confrontation. The very first thing most of us want to do when faced with something negative is to react. You might want to hit or yell or strike back in some way. But we have that split second where we can think about it. You don't always have to react when you're in a challenging situation. You can control that. You *cannot* control where and to whom you were born; you have no say over your environment or your parents or your race. But you *can* control your attitude.
>
> **C:** To be committed to anything, you first must be committed to yourself. Meaning you must be committed to telling the truth and to being honest, no matter how embarrassing or unpleasant the reality is.

E: It's actually simple to have enthusiasm. Start each day being glad for just having woken up, for being given another day. I am. I decide every morning that I am not going to walk around being negative. When I talk about the "E" in my definition of ACE, I say it loud, just like this: *Enthuuuuusssssssiasm.* Have it in everything you do.

LIFE

To me, LIFE means love, investment, family, and empowerment. Let me explain why those are important elements for having a happy and productive life.

L (Love): To love someone else, you must first love yourself. There is no possible way you can love someone else if you don't love *you*. Know yourself, accept yourself, and love yourself before you even think about sharing yourself. Deep down, we know who we are. We know our strengths and weaknesses. We must be honest with ourselves before true love can come in. And love is one of the most important parts of our lives. By the way, the best definition of love I have ever heard is that it is the consideration of everything and everybody.

I (Investment): Many people think investment means money. Sometimes it does, but in the definition of life, it means an investment in *you*. It means doing all you can to educate yourself, even if you don't have the means. You can surround yourself with people of character and learn and grow from them without spending a cent. Educate yourself, live honestly, and treat people how you want to be treated. This means investing in every part of you emotionally, physically, and mentally through education, self-improvement, and striving to complete your goals.

F (Family): We might have some crazy aunts and uncles or other family dynamics that make us want to avoid those holiday gatherings. Every family does, but blood is blood. If we can help in the betterment of our family members, we must do so. By family I also mean those people who we allow into our world. We must do all we can to help each member achieve success and reach whatever goals they have set for themselves.

E (Empowerment): I use this scenario often in my talks and presentations to youths and young adults. "A lot of you sit back and you don't do your chores. You don't take out the trash, and you don't do your homework. Correct?" I ask them. I hear some giggles, see some sheepish faces. Their parents nod. "When you're asked about it, you say, 'Well, you didn't tell me!' But you don't have to sit back and wait on someone to tell you to do it," I say. "You know what you need to do. It doesn't take someone else to empower you to do what you know you need to do."

My ultimate message is that they have the authority to empower themselves. And if we don't empower ourselves, we become average and ordinary.

87/10/3

Another philosophy I speak about often is the 87/10/3 rule. Basically, I believe these numbers, which of course add up to 100, reflect three distinct categories the world's population falls into.

Let me break that down for you.

87 percent of the world's population is average, ordinary, or below average, and they will live and think this way all their lives. They will do anything that someone asks them to, without question. They may complain about a request or job to their peers, but they have no real understanding of why they are doing it.

If, for example, they worked for a manufacturer that produced airplanes and their job was to produce fasteners to hold the skin or the metal surface of the airplane together, most of the 87-percenters would not be able to describe what they are building or the end goal of their work. Their only response would be that they are making fasteners because that's what the boss told them to do.

If someone told an 87-percenter to take a chair and walk around the factory five times, they would do it. If you asked them, "Why are you doing that?" their likely response would be, "Well, it's my job! I was asked to." If you don't know why you are doing something, you have the right to ask, "Why do you want me to do this? What is the purpose?"

10 percent are the movers and shakers. They want to understand what is being built, what the result of their work will be. As a 10-percenter they have to be able to come to the table with solutions. You've heard the term "thinking outside the box." That's this group.

They are also the ones to go against the status quo. If you were a manager and asked a 10-percenter to pick up a chair and walk around the building and sit the chair to the left of where it was before, they would probably think you were crazy and would argue with you.

But I'll come back to the 10 percent after I explain the 3-percenters.

3 percent are born wealthy, into a highly educated family or have a special gift. Most 3-percenters are always in the know. They understand revenue, management, profits, and most of the time are owners of, or in very high positions in, a company or organization.

They follow what I call the "golden rule." I'm sure you are familiar with that term, but to me it means "he who has the gold makes the rules." This group completely controls the other 97 percent of the world through power, wealth, tricking, and misleading them in some cases. It's very difficult to become a 3-percenter—but it is not impossible. The 87 percent may never become 3-percenters because they aren't focused that way unless they hit the lotto. Most of the 10-percenters will fight every situation with their boss because they don't understand the assignments or don't like what is being asked of them. These people will spend most of their lives challenging the ideas of others.

But I believe 1 percent of the 10 percent will go on to become a 3-percenter because instead of arguing with their boss or company about a given task that may not make sense, they will have the courage to ask the boss, "What do you really need done? What is your vision and outcome of what you are asking? Just tell me the end result and allow me to do it my way."

Let's go back to the example with the chair. One percent of the 10-percenter says to his boss, "Instead of walking around the building five times, just tell me where you want the chair." The boss points to his left, and the 10-percenter picks up the chair and moves it three feet to the left, saving the company millions of dollars just by asking the right question.

So strive to be among the one percent of the 10-percenters or even the 3-percenters. Why not? But it won't happen by dreaming small. You must dream big think big, be big, and aspire to be great In everything you do. You just never know where it will take you.

A STRONG FOUNDATION

I must start this philosophy, about building a strong foundation, by going back to my previous sayings about the 4 C's—create, collaborate, commit with confidence—which I believe are essential to establishing and maintaining a strong foundation.

Let's start with *create*. To me, create means all the things we want to do, all the goals we can see in our minds and want to complete. It's the way we envision our lives in the future. And I want us to have hope that someday we will see in front of us all of the ideas that were once only in our minds.

Collaborate in this context means that sometimes we may have ideas or dreams but doubt ourselves and think that we are different from others. Many of us will not share our ideas out of fear of rejection. But a key component to a strong foundation is collaboration. Often, we find others with similar thoughts and dreams as ours. If you collaborate with others who are likeminded, you can usually build a stronger plan to reach your goals and have these shared dreams come to life.

Commitment is the third key point to building a strong foundation. Once you commit to a dream, you must stay committed to your plan and process. I remember seven years ago when I dreamt one day of having a nonprofit organization to provide avenues to help our youths of today become the leaders of tomorrow. As I shared earlier, I spoke extensively with Don Dickson, who believed in me and my dream 100 percent. But I also met others along that journey who had a similar dream in developing a nonprofit. But their dreams did not match my vision. Therefore, I had to break away from them—but not from my commitment to establishing a nonprofit. Ultimately, I teamed up with Don and my wife, Michelle, to create The JC Cooley Foundation–Options & Opportunities: The Choice Program. My point is that regardless of what others may think, if you are committed to your dreams, DO IT. You can do anything if you build a strong foundation.

The fourth component is *confidence*. Remember—create, collaborate, commit with confidence. Once we understand that, we can set our minds on achieving our goals and bringing our visions to fruition. Using the 4 C's gives us the confidence to do anything, to be ourselves, and to accomplish things we could only have dreamed of.

So never lose confidence in yourself. Never surround yourself with pessimistic people, and never surround yourself with people you can't learn from. It's just a waste of time. No matter how successful we become, we must keep expanding our knowledge base and keep learning. Years ago, I decided that if I cannot learn something from you, I'm just not going to associate with you. If we surround ourselves with people we can't gain knowledge from, we won't grow.

And we want our knowledge base to be as big as it can get. That's how we build a strong foundation upon which we can pursue our destiny.

A START AND A FINISH DATE

Before I get too far into this chapter, I want to explain my definition of destination and destiny, which I believe have distinctly different meanings.

Every project we are given, every path we take, every journey we seek out to explore has a start and a finish date. Every destination we are on, including our very own lives, has a start and a finish date. And life is a series of destinations that keep us on our path to one day reaching our destiny.

When we enter high school, for example, our goal is to finish in four years or less. I call this our early destination. (Remember, I said destination, not destiny.) We must complete this destination to reach our next *destination*, be it college, military service, or entering the workforce, to gain life lessons and the building blocks needed to reach our *destiny*.

These building blocks are vision, understanding, and focus, which you will remember me discussing in a previous chapter. As we grow and mature, we sharpen our vision on what we want to become. We reduce some of the mistakes that we made earlier in life because we gained knowledge from our decisions, both the good and bad. Therefore, our understanding increases. But for us to continue to grow, we must remain focused.

And to accomplish our goals and reach our destiny in whatever time we have been given, we also must have short-term, mid-term, and long-term plans.

I told this to a group of student leaders during a presentation at Chaparral High School in Temecula during the spring of 2018. I spoke to all of them, at every grade level, but had pointed messages for the graduating seniors.

"Seniors, your high school destination ends in May," I said. "But if you have not planned on your next destination, you've got some problems. Because come May, life becomes different.

"Right now, you are on what I call a destination," I continued. "Your four years of high school are a destination. You have to be strong enough and focused enough to figure out when it's time to get off that proverbial train and know when the ride is coming to an end. You don't want to get too comfortable and miss your stop. You don't want to catch yourself saying, 'I know I finished high school, but if I fail this class, I can stay another semester.'"

Bottom line: You had better finish up your classes and jump off that train because life has got something else in store for you.

So how do we reach our destiny? Through a lifetime of learning and gaining knowledge and creating a foundation as big as we can get it—and through focus, which is key to our successes and to fulfilling our dreams.

Remember, a series of destinations leads us to our destiny. Where will your paths lead you?

We must find the uniqueness that is within every one of us to stay on track to reach our destiny. Not our destination, our destiny. Oftentimes we are walking down that path and we get sidetracked and thrown off course. Sometimes we get too comfortable and decide this is where we need to be. But go back to your foundation, which I hope you will build as big as you can. Go back to your uniqueness.

The Lord has remade me. He has given me focus on my destination, and along the way he brought me to you all. This is not by chance. I do not believe in anything by chance. This is what I told a group at a Trinity Speaker's Forum, a Christian organization, in Temecula.

Each of us has our own purpose, a path we must reach the end of, a destiny we must fulfill. Follow and complete your own destiny. That may take a lifetime.

As for me, I know I'm still on my path. I haven't reached my finish date. It ain't over yet.

THE CHOICE

Each of us must make our own *choice* about the path we will take. We are born with all the tools at birth—remember the birthrights: confidence, courage, hope, belief, and most importantly faith.

This leads us to the choice that is our destiny in life. We must consult with our Lord and Savior on all decisions we make as it relates to this choice.

Our Lord and Savior will provide the guidance and direction to us according to his plan. Once we receive His guidance, we can continue on our path knowing that our decisions are based on His direction. We should be thrilled and grateful but most importantly honored with the choice and our conviction to this choice to seek God's guidance.

We are born with the choice that we ultimately make; it is already instilled in us. We either enter this world crying instantly, or we may enter without a sound, needing help (a spank) to spark our first cry. These options are truly how you enter this world, so the choice is fully up to each individual soul, which is unique to them. Options lead to opportunities or potential successes, and opportunities lead us to making the right choice. This choice helps us create the roadmap to pursue our destiny.

PSSSSST...
YOU ARE A MASTERPIECE

You are a masterpiece, magnificently, fearfully, and wonderfully made. No one else is like you. Your creator broke the mold when you were made.

As stated in the King James Version of the Bible, "Trust in the Lord with all thine heart; and lean not unto thine own understanding. In all thy ways acknowledge him, and he shall direct thy paths."

The Lord made each one of us in His own image and with all the same birthrights—confidence, courage, hope, belief, and faith. But God also gave us something unique that I call our "secret sauce." No two people have the same secret sauce, not even twins. This makes every last one of us a masterpiece.

The situation or circumstance you have been born into does not matter because we all have the ability to rise beyond that and become who God intended for us to be.

It is up to us to discover the true purpose within us that God created for us. To do that, we must know ourselves—the good, the bad, and the ugly—and be truthful to who we are. We must continue to search within us, talk with God regularly, and, most importantly, never let others make us think that we are anything less than a masterpiece.

Once you know who you are—truly know who you are—accept yourself. Then love who you are, regardless of what anyone might say or think about you.

I'll tell you, these steps have allowed me to be me. They have allowed me to be the person God created me to be. They have allowed me to share myself with others by being the same true person every single day. This knowledge has allowed me to stay on track to complete this portion of my destination and continue moving toward my ultimate destiny.

And I—just like each one of you—am a masterpiece with my own "secret sauce" and destiny.

PART VI

REFLECTIONS:
Yesterday, Today, and Tomorrow

Recently, I had the tremendous opportunity to return to Chattanooga and speak at my fortieth class reunion. This happened as I was finishing writing this book. The timing seemed to be too perfect for me, allowing me to now share some of my reflections from seeing old classmates and reliving memories from 1978.

To the crowd of once familiar faces and names, some of which I hadn't heard or seen in decades, I said, "I must admit, our senior class was absolutely wonderful. We were a tight-knit group that loved the things we did with one another. The beginning of our senior year, as I remember, we were coming off a semi-state win for our football team that had a tremendous season finishing twelve and one, almost making it to the championship. That happened during my junior year, which I consider our most productive year in Kirkman Technical High School history. This team was led by some Kirkman Technical High School members who are here today."

Me and Michelle with my best friend Billy Harper and his wife Pamela before attending my 40th high school class reunion where I had the honor of being the keynote speaker (December 2018)

I continued, "I would like to recognize some of our great '78 classmates: Ken Hammock, Ron Jones, Charles Lanes, Billy Harper, Greg Crum, Efrin Stewart, Tim Newsom, and many, many others on the '78 Hawk football team who I don't recall right now, but your contribution is so important to today's reunion. Our basketball team consisted of some of our great guys. Remember our junior year, when we had all-senior starters led by Larry Aiken and other upperclassmen? I remember when the senior starters decided to quit the team for some unknown reason, which led our class to step up and finish our junior basketball team, which [was] led by some of our current Hawks here tonight. [Those players] learned a lot from this adversity with all of our senior members quitting for different reasons over basketball coaching disagreements. As juniors playing on a team of a four and zero record prior to our senior players deciding to call it quits, our Hawks stepped up."

My point in writing this last part of my book is that I was reminded how I was voted "Most Likely to Succeed" and also "Class Clown" along with Anthony Knox. It is my understanding, after seeing and chatting with Anthony on the night before our fortieth reunion, that he was very successful in a twenty-year Army career. I believe many of our '78 classmates are also very successful, and I am so happy for them.

I was also so happy and humbled to be the keynote speaker for our reunion and to see so many of my classmates I had not seen or talked to in decades.

I made sure to carefully choose the right message for them—LIFE or "love, investment, family, and empowerment." I chose to speak about this because I believe that my hometown is still in a generational time warp. I don't believe that it or many of the mindsets there have changed much over the last forty years. It is up to us, the Class of '78, to set the example by educating ourselves and being role models for our children and grandchildren and to be focused on our next generation. We must understand and remember what happened to our class during our basketball season and our generation. We must remember our successes and our failures. We must remember them, however, but we must not live in the past. We must realize that we are living in different situations and circumstances today, and we must be able to adapt to change based on today's technology and progress and be willing to accept all people based on love and not prejudice.

We must learn from the past, but not live it. We must live in the present, today, but most importantly, we must always prepare for tomorrow.

We must place our primary focus on ensuring that we are prepared to be ready to lead or provide positive influence for our future leaders of tomorrow. I was so honored that my 1978 Kirkman Technical High School class believed that I was living that example.

And to my readers, thank you so much for reading my book. Every word exhibits my vision, understanding, and focus (VUF, as I call it) of how I believe we should live, we should lead, and most importantly, where our focus should be to help guide and mold our youths to become future leaders.

ACKNOWLEDGMENTS

First and foremost, I would like to thank my Lord and Savior Jesus Christ. I also must thank John Kohler, my publisher, who believed in my story and gave me an opportunity to tell it.

I owe a special acknowledgment to my brothers Jerry Cooley and Joe Askew and my very good friend who was like a big sister to me during my teenage years, Sandra Harper-Jones. I miss you so much

I also want to say thanks to my other brothers and sisters: Mary Hadyen, Rosemary Stephens, Robert Cooley, Willie Cooley, Gaylo Jo Suttles, Gary Stephens, and my baby brother Jonathan Holloway. Without you, none of the memories would have been possible.

Most importantly, I thank my beautiful wife Michelle Cooley for providing the inspiration to keep me motivated and grounded day to day. To my four children, James III, Deangelo, Brittany and Joshua: You are my heart and help keep me focused on today's and tomorrow's challenges.

I owe a debt of gratitude to all the great people I have encountered in my life who helped me develop into the person I am today and who inspired me to Dream Big, Think Big, and most importantly, Be Big. And I can't forget the many folks I see every day at my gym, the 24

Hour Fitness in Temecula, California. I look forward to seeing these great Americans ("my peeps" as I call them). You guys are the greatest!

One, Don Dickson, inspired me to write "My Path" and "The Book of Knowledge" and this current writing. To my very good friend Charles Golden, a big thank you for supporting the JC Cooley Foundation. You are a great executive vice president and business partner, and I love you my friend! Others who encouraged me along my journey include: Dan Goodwin, Charles May, Charles Stewart, my junior high school teacher Mrs. Brown, my elementary school principal Mr. White, Navy Retired Captain Lillian Peoples, Captain Charles Cooper, Lt. Commander Vince Cromer, Captain Synthia Jones, CW04 William Hardman, Captain Joy (USS Blue Ridge CO), Lt. Commander William Harris (OIC Moffett Field), Commander William Stamper (OIC Misawa Japan), RADM Arthur Johnson (RADM), Lillian Fishburne (first black female PAC Admiral in the U.S. Navy), Marlynne Cooley, Gwen Wright, Sandy Dodson, Jackie Grossman (always happy), Navy Retired Captain Greg Copeland, Navy Retired Commander Bernadette Semple, Navy Retired Captain Herman Archilbald, Garret Durian, Peggy Gagon, Jim Burgess, Frank Lowe, Salvador Jimenerz, Guy Chirco, Jacob Brown, Kory Agianes, Charles Gore, Morton Hayden, Norman Blevins, Ernest Blevins, Lyssa Stanton, Jim Burgess, Jim Willis, Billy Harper, Franciso Villa, Jose Suarez, Bob Nanigian (the mouth), Jackie Grossman, Steve Taylor (my very good friend) who was one of the original members of the JC Cooley Foundation, John Barger, my first cousin Genice Green who provided much documentation and many of the family pictures shown in this book, my niece Shantal Hardin and so many more names that should be mentioned in this book. Thank you all.

A final note of appreciation must go to Katie Ismael. I consider you a "gatekeeper" who I believe God sent into my life to place me on the right path to focus on writing this book. Not only did you encourage me, you were also the inspiration in transcribing my story into this beautiful manuscript that our readers are enjoying today.

We spent many hours together where I shared my background and my philosophies, and you listened; you heard my words and then helped shape them into a story that I hope others will take with them on their own journeys.

Katie, I haven't the words to say or describe how grateful I am to have Michelle and you in my life. No way I could have done this without you. Thank you so much my friend.

Each one of you has helped me come to this final thought I want to leave my readers: We all create our own path, our own direction in our quest to be successful in life. This is my story, one of a city boy and country boy whose journey ain't over yet. And our journey does not end until we allow it to be over.

I am blessed.

The back yard of the house where I grew up in Graham, Alabama (1968)

A current photo of the barn and chicken house of our property where I grew up in Graham, Alabama. My family no longer owns the land.

Receiving a Navy commendation medal from Commander Rundebursch, Royal Australian Navy Executive Officer, prior to me leaving Exmouth, Australia (1980)

The Exmouth United States Pro Basketball League Championship, my team in 1983

Me (far left) playing in the Worldwide Lemond Cup in Sydney, Australia where I was voted outstanding player of the tournament (1984)

Receiving a Navy Achievement Medal from Lieutenant Commander Harris, Officer in Charge Moffit Field, California (1987)

Sailor of the Year in Guam (1989)

Keeping in shape to maintain my title as the Midwest bodybuilding and weightlifting champion at the 186-weight class (1993)

I'm hanging out with Run (of the famous 1980s hip hop group Run-D.M.C.) on tour in Yokusuka, Japan (1995). (I, indeed, met some interesting and famous folks when I dabbled in comedy and acting.)

My oldest son, James Cooley III, and my daughter, Brittany Cooley, at our home in Masawa, Japan (1995)

My first speech after being sworn in as a United States Navy Ensign on board the USS Blueridge (19) (January 1995)

Standing by to assume the commanding officer position as the Officer in Charge of the Naval Command Communication Detachment in Misawa, Japan (March 1995)

A photo of my unit in Misawa, Japan selected to be shown on "Good Morning America" in 1996

Don Dickson (center), Steve Taylor and me before my first speech to the Temecula Old Town Rotary Club. Steve and Don are original supporters of the JC Cooley Foundation and were with me from the beginning on that journey (November 2014)

The California Democratic Party endorsement of me, Hillary Clinton and Kamala Harris among others in the 2016 election

Speaking to a class at Temecula's Chaparral High School about how to achieve my 4Cs (2018)

Michelle and me with my youngest son, Josh, on his graduation day from Palomar Community College in San Marcos, California, 2018. He entered the California State University system to earn his bachelor's degree that fall.

Me and Mayor James Stewart before I presented four scholarships to area high school students at the 2019 Temecula Dollars for Scholars

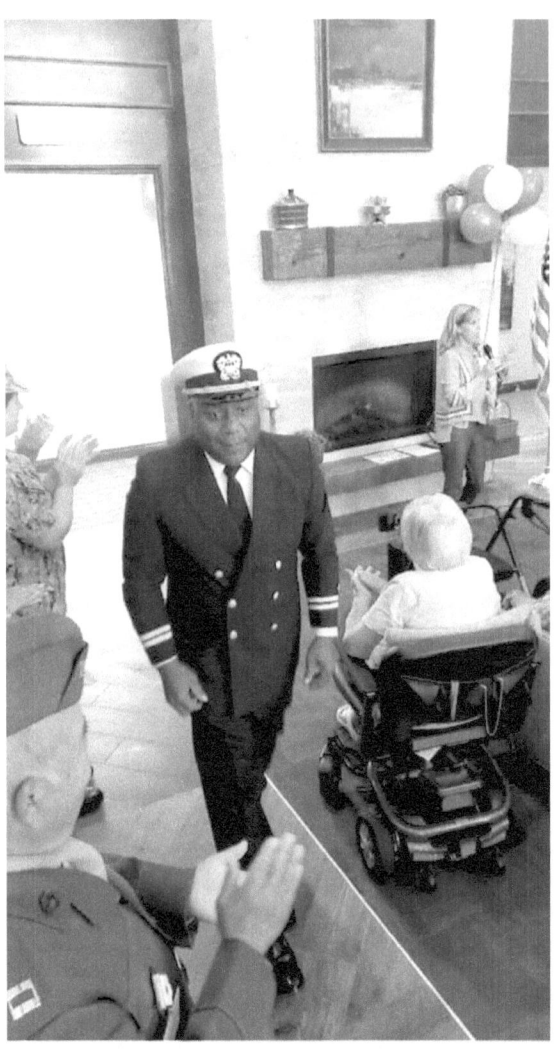

I was given the opportunity to speak to World War Two and Korean War Veterans celebrating the 74th Anniversary of WWII at the Vineyard Ranch Nursing Home in Temecula (August 2019)

www.ingramcontent.com/pod-product-compliance
Lightning Source LLC
Chambersburg PA
CBHW030525080526
44586CB00011B/319